Eternity Beckons

Are You Ready?

By
Richard Smart

Copyright © 2022. Published by Etheal Publishing.

No part of this publication may be reproduced, stored in a retrieval system or transmitted in any form or by any means, electronic, mechanical, photocopying, recording, scanning or otherwise, except as permitted under Sections 107 or 108 of the 1976 United States Copyright Act, without the prior written permission of the Author. Requests to the Author for permission should be addressed to: richcorrol@gmail.com

Limit of Liability/Disclaimer of Warranty: The Publisher and the Author make no representations or warranties with respect to the accuracy or completeness of the contents of this work and specifically disclaim all warranties, including without limitation warranties of fitness for a particular purpose. No warranty may be created or extended by sales or promotional materials. The advice and strategies contained herein may not be suitable for every situation. This work is sold with the understanding that both the Publisher and the Author are not engaged in rendering legal, pastoral or other professional advice or services. If professional assistance is required, the services of a competent professional or ecclesiastical person should be sought. Neither the Publisher nor the Author shall be liable for damages arising herefrom. The fact that an individual, organisation or website is referred to in this work as a citation and/or potential source of further information does not mean that the Author or the Publisher endorses the information the individual, organisation or website may provide or recommendations they/it may make.

Unless otherwise indicated, all Scripture quotations are taken from the King James Version and the New King James Version®. Copyright © 1982 by Thomas Nelson. Used by permission. All rights reserved.

Final Editing & Formatting:
L Rimmer

Interior and Cover Designer:
Etheal Publishing

ISBN: Print 9780951347522

First published in 2022.

All rights reserved.

Eternity Beckons

ETHEAL PUBLISHING

Acknowledgements

I would like to thank my friends and family who have stood with me and helped me with this book, particularly my wife. For many years she has stood with me and supported me and enabled me to learn many things.

I would also like to thank those who took time to proof read and help with the book.

But above all else, I give the glory to God. I thank Him for all He has done for me.

Endorsements

"Eternity Beckons is a must read for every Christian who is looking at understanding how passion and faith can make us do much more than we are doing today. I am honoured and humbled to write about a person I have known personally for over 20 years and seen the passion and love for Christ that drives him beyond all odds to work for eternity. Richard Smart is a person who inspires one to borrow his unique perception of Eternity. I have walked closely and can attest to his great desire for missions, sharing the word, desire for the church to be equipped through reading books and any practical ways of helping the poor through creating employment opportunities for everyone he can reach out to. His life remains a great testimony of what God can make out of a person who dedicates his life to fully serve the Lord and he shares this in this amazing book. Special thanks to his dear wife who has allowed him come a long way to provide a great spiritual resource to the body of Christ."

- Jimmy Bodo, CEO Legacy Trust Uganda

"Richard writes with a heart felt honesty and enthusiasm. This crucial area cannot be emphasised enough, and Richard's book is an invaluable addition to the understanding of eternity and eternal life. His illustrations and examples are well drawn and relevant as well as being challenging to all professing Christians. Read this book and it will be both a blessing to you and a means of blessing others regarding this topic of utmost importance."

- Paul Board, BSc Econ (Hons)

"Richard raises some important topics for Christians to consider – how can we be extraordinarily fruitful in our walk with the Lord and how can we reap a hundredfold harvest for His Kingdom in the

things we do in our day-to-day lives? In the blink of an eye, this life will be over and we'll be into eternity. Since all that we do for the Lord now will reap an eternal reward, whilst those things we do not do for Him are burnt up as stubble, should we not seek to maximise our work, time and devotion to Him? This book is thought provoking, challenging and will prompt you to reprioritise things in light of eternity beckoning. I know Richard has a deep desire to see the Church awake, watchful, devoted and mature – awaiting the Lord's return for her."

- J.L. Fuller, Author 'Romans 13 and Covid 19 – Knowledge, Warnings and Encouragement for the Church and World'

This book reveals the heart of the writer, to see people come to know the love of God. It is unique in its field, full of questions we all need to answer before leaving earth, and many personal stories to bless the reader. If you already know your eternal life in heaven is secure, why not give it to a friend who needs to find out, because eternity beckons.....Loving Shalom.

- Brenda Taylor, Dovetail Shalom

Preface

The love of God is deeper than anyone can understand. No one can comprehend it. No one. It is so deep. And it's wonderful for every one of us to be loved by God. It really is.

In Ephesians 3 we read: 'that you may be able to comprehend with all the saints what is the width and length and depth and height—to know the love of Christ which passes knowledge; that you may be filled with all the fullness of God.' Ephesians 3v18-19 NKJV. The love of God is beyond what we know. It is so deep. It's so wonderful. It passes knowledge. God loves us with an everlasting love. And the good news is that God can never stop loving us here on earth, because God *is* love.

But what does this mean? When a parent loves their child, does that mean that the child can do anything they like and the parent will always give them a hug? What if a child says to their parent, "I did something wrong today at school and the teacher never found out. I'm so glad I was not caught." Does the parent hug their child and say 'well done', or do they ask the child what they did in the school that was wrong and tell them not to do it again? Are you pleased if your child is bad, or do you discipline the child so that they will do their best to be good all the time?

What does it mean to be loved by God? Can we also be bad all the time and rest assured of the fact that God loves us too? Can we be lazy and still rest assured knowing that we are always loved by God? Can we ignore the scriptures, forget about the Word of God and enjoy the fact that God loves us all the time? Could God be passionate to discipline us in any way? Could there be any consequences if we are reluctant to change for God? What does it mean to be loved by God? What does it mean, both on earth and for eternity?

Look at one verse in the Bible. Revelation 3v19 says, "As many as I love, I rebuke and chasten. Therefore be zealous and repent." This verse may seem very odd and strange. How can a loving God decide to rebuke and chasten a person? Surely if you love someone, you accept them as they are. You don't begin to rebuke them. You love them just the way they are. We may like to think this way, but does a parent really love a child just the way they are and never make any effort to teach them what is good and right? Does a parent always say 'yes' to a child when they go shopping and a child asks for sweets or toys? What if every parent said 'yes' all the time and apologised in the home that there was no food to eat because they decided to buy toys all the time for the children? Would a child feel sad if they were hungry and had no food to eat? I'm sure they would. It's not nice to find yourself hungry and have nothing to eat.

There are times when parents will discipline and say 'no' to things so that a child is able to always have a good meal and grow to become a healthy adult. Does God, our heavenly Father, have the opportunity to discipline us too? Or do we only want to see the nice side of God, his love and kindness, and forget about his rebuking and chastening?

I trust that this book will draw us all to a beautiful relationship with God. I pray that we will learn how we can have a very wonderful relationship with God and know Him more and more. And I pray that our lives in heaven will be so rich and beautiful. Our life in eternity is much longer than our life on earth, and I long to see not only people entering heaven but also many eternal treasures too.

Remember, every Father likes to talk to their children, and God delights to talk to us. May the Lord reveal many things to you through this book so that you enjoy a lovely, intimate relationship with Him.

Richard Smart

Eternity Beckons – Are You Ready?

Contents

Acknowledgements 4
Endorsements 5
Preface 7
PART 1: LIVING FOR ETERNITY 12
CHAPTER 1 - HOW CAN YOU QUANTIFY LOVE? 13
CHAPTER 2 - WHAT IS A CHRISTIAN? 23
CHAPTER 3 - THE WORD OF GOD 31
CHAPTER 4 – ETERNAL TREASURES 40
CHAPTER 5 – THE HEART 47
CHAPTER 6 – THE CHURCH 54
CHAPTER 8 – GOD'S MEASURING ROD 79
CHAPTER 9 - OWNING A CAR: THE LAW AND FREEDOM 98
PART 2: REVELATIONS FROM GOD 116
CHAPTER 10 – A WRONG INTERPRETATION OF HUMILITY AND UNITY 119
CHAPTER 11 - OUR FIRST LOVE 128
CHAPTER 12 – A WRONG DEFINITION OF LOVE 135
CHAPTER 13 – QUICK TO ACCUSE OTHERS 139
CHAPTER 14 – APOSTLES AND PROPHETS 144
CHAPTER 15 – PLEASING GOD ABOVE MAN 157
CHAPTER 16 – LOVING OTHERS 164
CHAPTER 17 – CONCLUSION 171
About the Author 178

Part 1:
Living for Eternity

Chapter 1 – How Can You Quantify Love?

"I always knew I should never have married you. You didn't really love me at all. You always sit in front of the TV and leave me to do everything. I'm separating from you and never going to see you ever again. You're not going to make me change my mind."

How does a marriage work? What has to be done to make sure it lasts and never ends? How does one feel when they are suddenly told something they never expected to hear?

What does it mean to love God? What has to be done to be sure one is honouring God all the time? How would one feel to be suddenly told on judgment day by Jesus, "Depart from me? I never knew you"?

Imagine a couple are getting married very soon. They are going to a place for marriage guidance as they prepare for their wedding. The first thing they are told is about the importance of love. A marriage is all about a relationship based on love. And they are asked a question. 'Do you want to love the other one forever and ever? Do you always want to be a blessing to the other one?'

Love is very important in a relationship. When something goes wrong, you don't immediately say, "I'm leaving you. This marriage is over." You love each other and seek a solution. You find a way to deal with the problem. The couple remind themselves about the importance of loving one another all the time.

So how does someone define the way a husband should love his wife? If a husband says twice a day to his wife "I love you", does that prove that he really is a husband? If he says to her, "I love you" twice each day and he makes her a hot cup of tea each morning, is that evidence that he really loves her? What about if he does this, goes to work, and comes home in the evening and cleans the house? Does that prove, absolutely prove beyond doubt, that he loves her? If so, does that give him the right to listen to the radio at night with the volume on at maximum? The wife gently says to her husband, 'please can you turn the volume down as I want to rest and it is very loud.' How can a husband react? He can respect her and turn the volume down or even turn the radio off. Or he can respond saying, "I've been at work all day. I make you a hot cups of tea. Please can you let me do what I want? Please don't tell me what to do." Can he have his own way at night because of all his hard work during the day?

What does a husband have to do every day to ensure he pleases his wife and she does not leave him? She appreciates his kind words and the hot drinks he gives her. She is full of gratitude and thanks. But she struggles to tolerate the unpleasantness every night. He seems to enjoy music in the late hours of the night and it's hard to sleep with all the noise in the home.

The husband, on the other hand, does not want exclusion. Two other men at work also listen to the radio at night time and talk about the things that they heard on the radio. This man does not want to miss out on things, so he also wants to have the radio on. But there is one very big difference in the lives of the men. The other two men each have a wife who work regularly nights in the local hospital from 10pm to 6am, so both men are alone in the house at night. They can have the radio on and no one else is disturbed. This man, however, is at home with his wife. He has to consider how she feels.

How do you ensure a marriage will always work out? How do you quantify love? The truth is, you cannot. You come to learn when someone loves you and respects you all the time and also when they are stubborn and refuse to change their ways. Love cannot be quantified. No husband can say, "If I do six good deeds for you every day then you have to allow me to have all my friends in the home every night for loud music and alcohol." A lot of good deeds cannot justify a beautiful marriage when a person then decides to do something every night that brings a lot of sadness to his wife. A husband who may only say "I love you" to his wife once a day, every night before they rest, but who always respects her and never wants to offend her may be more gentle and loving than one who says "I love you" twice a day but still puts the radio on in the night and makes a lot of noise.

Can you measure the length of time it takes, in minutes and seconds, for a cup of coffee to get cold? If you are in a hotel and are served a hot cup of coffee, do you think that after thirty seconds it will be cold? No. It is still very hot. However, you may decide to leave the hot cup of coffee on the table, go for a swim for one hour and then return to the table. Do you think the cup of coffee will still be hot? Or will it be cold? It will have cooled down and become very cold. You may not want the drink anymore now that it has turned cold.

Now the question is, at what point did it become cold? After 4 minutes and 10 seconds, or 8 minutes and 20 seconds? At what point? If you asked twenty people to make a cup of coffee and measure the length of time it takes for the coffee to become cold, you may end up with twenty different answers. A person may say that a cup of coffee is nearly cold, but another may wait until they can say, for absolute certainty, that the coffee is definitely cold. How do you define when it is cold? Do you need to get a thermometer and measure the temperature of the drink? Or can you use your common sense and tell when it is cold?

The greatest commandment in the Bible is all about love. The command is to 'love' the Lord your God with all your heart. And the Bible talks about temperatures. Look at these two scriptures:

"So then, because you are lukewarm, and neither cold nor hot, I will vomit you out of My mouth." Revelation 3v16 NKJV

"And because lawlessness will abound, the love of many will grow cold." Matthew 24v12 NKJV

How can you define when a church is lukewarm? How can you quantify when the love inside a person is now cold as Matthew 24 says? There is no precise way to say when a church is lukewarm or when the love of someone has grown cold. You discern, after a period of time, where the church is, and where the heart of the person is. A person in a church may be still as passionate as ever towards those they love, or may have become discouraged in some way and are not as devoted as they once were. They even feel like withdrawing. 'Their love has grown cold', you might say.

At other times a person's love may not be growing cold at all. Someone may simply be choosing to move to another place where they can be of greater blessing to others. We have to discern the heart of the person before we respond. Some hearts may grow cold, but others move on because they believe there are things to do in another place and God is opening a door for them. Paul told the people in Ephesus that he would not see them again – Acts 20v38. Does that mean that his love for the people grew cold? No. He simply believed the time had come to move to another town, and so he moved on to other places to continue to teach the scriptures.

How can you tell if a husband really loves his wife? How can you tell if a person really loves God with all their heart? How can you tell when a person's love has grown cold? You have to get to know the person and their ways in order to understand them.

The question we all have to ask ourselves is this. "Is my life a blessing to God?" Notice we are not asking, "is my life a blessing to the church?" but "is my life a blessing to God?" God is our judge, and one day we will all appear before the judgment seat to give an account of ourselves before Him. Did our love grow cold? Was God telling us to repent because we had lost our first love? Or were we a blessing to God all the time? What will God say on judgment day?

Now let's ask another question. Can you quantify how long a good ministry is? How long do we have to stay in one place before God moves us on? Let's again look at Paul.

"Therefore watch, and remember that *for three years* I did not cease to warn everyone night and day with tears." Acts 20v31 NKJV

How long was Paul with the people in Ephesus? He was with them for three years.

Paul loved the people of Ephesus very much. He longed to see them know God's ways. He did not want them to turn away from God. He was passionate for them to follow God all the time. Do we therefore say that ministry should be in one place for three years and then someone moves on? Do we follow the example of Paul?

Look at a university. A student may begin a University course for three years and then graduate. Consider some alternative ways of living as a university student. Can a degree be completed in three months instead of three years? Or can a degree last for thirty years instead of three years? University life can be very nice, seeing so many other students and enjoying activities together such as football, running or cycling, so it would be great if a degree could be for thirty years instead of three years. But if everyone spent so many years in education, who would ever go to work? Who would teach in a Primary School or work in a supermarket? No one wants to work because everyone likes to study all the time. How would we ever be able to buy food if no one wants to work in a supermarket or be a driver and deliver the food to the shops? Three years may therefore be a good number of years to study and get a degree so that a student learns a lot and is ready to get a good job and earn a good income. People go to work in a society instead of continually studying, and things get done because people are working.

But is three years the set number for someone to do something? Should someone lead a church for three years then move on? Again, let's look at Paul.

And Paul after this tarried there yet a good while. Acts 18v18

It does not say how many months or years Paul was in Corinth. And yet Acts 20v31 specifically says how long Paul was in Ephesus. So we see a difference. One verse is specific, but another is not. Can you always quantify the length of service you give to a group of people? Clearly the Bible shows that you cannot always give a specific period of time. Does that, therefore, give us justification to stay in one place for a very long period of time? We can always defend ourselves constantly quoting these two verses, Acts 20v31 and Acts 18v18. But the question is, are we using our brain to work out things, or are we looking at things from the heart? What is the motive of our decisions, our intellect or our heart?

Just how do you define things? Look at these two verses:

The Bible says:

"Pursue peace with all people, and holiness, without which no one will see the Lord." Hebrews 12v14 NKJV

"But without faith it is impossible to please God." Hebrews 11v6 NKJV

How do you quantify 'holiness'? How do you quantify 'faith'?

If I pray just one day a year and believe God will answer my prayer, am I exercising faith in God? I pray and ask that there will be no rain this afternoon when I go out for a walk. I prayed, I believed, and there was no rain. Am I therefore pleasing God because I have faith? How much faith do I need in order to please God?

If I pray just one day a year, am I being holy because I am praying to God? "Lord, please enable my friend to get a job. Amen." By praying just once a year, am I being holy? How do I measure my life to know, for sure, that I am being holy? Look at Luke 18:

The Pharisee stood and prayed thus with himself, 'God, I thank You that I am not like other men—extortioners, unjust, adulterers, or even as this tax collector. I fast twice a week; I give tithes of all that I possess.' And the tax collector, standing afar off, would not so much as raise *his* eyes to heaven, but beat his breast, saying, 'God, be merciful to me a sinner!' I tell you, this man went down to his house justified *rather* than the other; for everyone who exalts himself will be humbled, and he who humbles himself will be exalted." Luke 18v11-14 NKJV

The Pharisee felt he was right because he fasted twice a week. The fact that he fasted must have proved he was holy. He may not believe he needed to confess his sin. However, the tax collected did. He asked for mercy (verse 13). Surely the Pharisee was doing more for God than the tax collector. But listen to Jesus' words:

"I tell you that this man, rather than the other, went home justified before God. For all those who exalt themselves will be humbled, and those who humble themselves will be exalted." Luke 18v14 NKJV

Jesus said that the tax collector was the one justified before God, not the Pharisee. Jesus looked at their hearts, and the willingness of the tax collector to admit his sinful ways was more honouring to God than the Pharisee who was full of pride and boasting about himself. Pride is not a blessing to God at all. As James 4v6 says:

"God resists the proud, but gives grace to the humble." NKJV

Now let's compare the Apostle Paul in Acts 13 with Jesus in John 4.

Then Saul, who also is called Paul, filled with the Holy Spirit, looked intently at him and said, "O full of all deceit and all fraud, you son of the devil, you enemy of all righteousness, will you not cease perverting the straight ways of the Lord? Acts 13v9-10 NKJV

The woman said to Him, "I know that Messiah is coming" (who is called Christ). "When He comes, He will tell us all things." Jesus said to her, "I who speak to you am *He.*" John 4v25-26 NKJV

Paul confronted the darkness in the person. Why? Because the Holy Spirit lived in Paul and gave him both the words and the boldness to deal with the matter. The person was not willing to live in an honourable way but clung to an evil spirit. Jesus, on the other hand, showed love to the person, even though she had lived with five different husbands. He did not see an evil spirit in her but instead a soul that was searching for the truth. And he revealed himself to the lady. Paul (or rather the Holy Spirit in Paul), and Jesus reacted in very different ways. In one instance the dark spirit was confronted, and in the other the person was shown gentleness and love.

How should we be living? You cannot automatically say that a Christian who reads the Bible for twenty five minutes every day is more likely to grow stronger than someone who only reads their Bible for twenty minutes every day. Nor can you say that someone who attends five prayer meetings a week will have a stronger faith than someone who only attends four prayer meetings a week. The gospel is not just about the number of hours in which we do things every week. Christianity is far deeper than just attending meetings.

When we look into the Word of God and all the different things we read, we realise that there are many different ways that things are done. The whole purpose of this book is to look at many of the different ways that God speaks through the Bible and to know Him more and more. What is He saying, and how does it apply to us? Is there an eternal impact, and if so, what are the consequences of our choices? It's very easy to become intellectual and say things and draw our own conclusions in a situation. And yet, and as this chapter shows, some things cannot be precise. There is no precise number of minutes and seconds you can leave a cup of coffee on the table before it turns cold. And there is no exact or precise way you should use every hour of the day to live as a Christian.

If that is so, what should we do? Let's start by looking at what the gospel is really all about.

Chapter 2 - What is a Christian?

Exactly what do we have to do to escape hell and go to heaven? How do we make sure, when we die, we will enter heaven? Throughout this book you will see many questions. Each time, take time to pause and to think about what could be a healthy answer for our lives and for the situation.

We all want to go to heaven. No one wants to enter hell. So what do we have to do? Let's look at some possible answers.

Look at this verse. 2 Corinthians 5v7 says, "Therefore if any man be in Christ, he is a new creature: old things are passed away; behold, all things are become new."

'Old things are passed away' says the Bible. We stop living our old ways. But is this right? If someone used to be a generous neighbour before they became a Christian, should they stop being generous? The 'old' is gone, says the Bible, so should they change completely and stop being generous? Imagine having some cows and giving some free milk to your neighbours, and later you become a Christian. Do you have to stop being generous? What does it mean when the Bible says, "The old is gone"?

It means giving up things that do not please the Lord. Anything that is against his ways is sin. That is what we have to give up as we begin living a new life. The question is, 'how do we know what we have to give up?' The way to know for sure is to read the Bible and see what it says. What are God's ways? What does God like and dislike? We have to know the heart of God in order to get to know his ways and how to please Him. And as we do so, we discover that God loves someone with a generous heart, so we do not have to stop giving at all.

But, above all else, we have to know God. As we get to know His heart, we get to know Him more and more. We have a relationship with Him, and the more we know Him, the richer our relationship becomes.

The greatest commandment is to 'Love the Lord your God with all your heart.' Mark 12v30. Look at what the Bible does *not* say.

Love the Lord your God with *the majority of your heart* but not all your heart.

Love the Lord your God with *part of your heart* but not necessarily all of your heart.

The Bible does *not* say this.

God asks us to love Him with *all* our heart. For a husband to love his wife by saying "I love you" to her every day and making her a lovely hot cup of tea in the morning is not loving her with all his heart if he then forgets about her at night time and sits with the radio on at full volume. He is not respecting her 24 hours a day. At night time he thinks only of himself and forgets about her. Is he really loving his wife with all his heart? No. He may say he loves her and does not want her to leave him, but he does not respect her at night time. He does what he wants, for his own pleasure, and does not respect her when she asks for quietness in the home.

What if you or I choose to apply a fair amount of the Word of God in our lives, but not all the Word of God? Some things we decide we will *not* do, such as teaching God's Word to others as Hebrews 5v12 says. We would rather just attend church and be taught all the time. We don't want to start teaching others. Are we actually loving God with all our heart and respecting him in everything He asks us to do, or preferring to love Him with the majority of our heart but not all our heart?

It is possible that a wife could say, after a number of years of marriage to her husband, that she wants to end the relationship. "I know you love me. You tell me every day. But I have to say that I've reached a point where I simply cannot enjoy our marriage anymore. I feel unwanted when I go to bed every night because you will not turn down the volume on the radio. I go to bed very disheartened. No matter how much I say, you completely ignore me. The time has come for me to go to see a lawyer and arrange for a divorce."

Could God say, "Although you say you love me and want to please me, you will not repent when I tell you there is something in you that I do not like. I do not like you continually saying, in your prayers, how you hate that person and wish they were gone from the community. You give faithfully to the church every Sunday and help with the cleaning, but you are refusing to love one person and have deep hatred in your heart towards them. I cannot therefore give you eternal life."

What does 1 John say?

"Whosoever hates his brother is a murderer: and ye know that no murderer hath eternal life abiding in him." 1 John 3v15

The author, J L Fuller, says in the book, Romans 13 and Covid 19, that 'The essence of the Gospel is acknowledging Jesus as the God who became man and died for the sins of humanity and putting our faith in Him as our Saviour, Lord and King of our life. They go on to say, 'It's about a living, personal, intimate relationship with our Creator God.' *page 445*. 'It's about an intimate relationship' says the author. 'An intimate relationship with God.'

There are others who will think differently. Some may say that Christianity has nothing to do with a relationship. It's about conforming to church rules and learning to submit to your church leader. Let's imagine someone is out for a walk and they see an evangelist on the streets. They stop and listen to the evangelist and are told that Jesus can forgive all their sins right now, and are invited to give their life to Jesus. They say a prayer, saying sorry for their sins and asking Jesus to forgive them and come into their heart. The evangelist then tells them that they are now a Christian and should join a local church. 'Everyone needs to grow', the evangelist says, 'so find a church and join it. It will help you to grow in your Christian life.' The person respects the words of the evangelist and joins a local church. Having done so, they believe they are 'Christian.'

Volunteers are required in the church to help make refreshments after the service, so as a 'Christian' you learn to show loyalty to the church and help in different meetings. Christians are not meant to be lazy, and if everyone was lazy then nobody would do anything. "I'm not cleaning the church. I'm not making the teas and coffees. Others can do it. Not me." If everyone thought like this, no one would do anything, and we are taught to serve in the church and help others. So as long as we do what we are taught, surely we can know for sure that we are being Christian and no one can point the finger at us. "The evangelist told everyone to find a church to join, and I have done what I was told, so what right has anyone to judge me? I'm doing what I was told to do" we can say.

People could be regularly attending a church with such a mindset. They simply do not see anything wrong in the way they live and do not see the need for change in their lives. Regular church attendance is living proof that they are a Christian, and there are enough witnesses to prove it. People know that this person has been attending the same church for very many years, so there is absolutely no doubt that they are a committed Christian.

What's forgiveness got to do with being a Christian? What does it matter if I cannot forgive someone and still hate them every time I see them? The evangelist told me to join a church and I have done so, so how can anyone say I'm not being a Christian? Therefore, if a person regularly attends a church then they can 'prove' they are a Christian in the same way that a Muslim is one who regularly attends a mosque.

However, there are others who may say that the only requirement to be a Christian is to believe in Jesus. Look at this verse.

"For God so loved the world, that he gave his only begotten Son, that whosoever believeth in him should not perish, but have everlasting life." John 3v16 NKJV

This verse refers to everlasting life. What that is referring to is life after earth. Once we die here on earth, the Bible says that there are two places we can go to, either heaven or hell. And John 3v16 says that whoever 'believes' in him, Jesus, shall have everlasting life. So, as long as someone believes in Jesus, they know that when they die they will go to heaven. They do not have to attend a church and be part of a church family. To believe is sufficient to get into heaven.

But what does it actually mean? Does it mean that someone explains what 'Good Friday' is and why it is a public holiday, and I believe what they say? If I believe that someone called Jesus really did get nailed to a cross and die, then I believe the story about the death of Jesus and so I will go to heaven when I die. I'm sure the story of Jesus dying on the cross is true. I'm sure it is. So, because I believe, can I be absolutely sure that when I die I will go to heaven? That's what John 3v16 says. "Everyone who believes in him will have eternal life." Great. It's so easy. Just hear the story of what Good Friday is all about, believe it and you will go to heaven. Very simple.

Let's again look at John 3v16. It does not say, 'believe and repent.' It does not say 'believe and forgive.' It does not say 'believe and join a church.' It just says, 'believe.' If that's what the Bible says, then belief is all that is required. A person can believe and have an unforgiving heart towards their neighbour. John 3v16 does not say you have to forgive. All it says it that you have to believe. A person does not have to join a church or repent of their sins. If someone wants to have a birthday and invite their brother but not their sister then they can do what they like. 'I don't have to invite my sister as she stole my pen all those years ago and never gave it back to me. I can exclude her from every event I host and invite my parents and brothers but not her. I can do as I wish, and I know I'm going to heaven because I'm a believer. And even if I lie about my sister, saying that she keeps stealing my pens from me whenever she comes to my home, I know I'll go to heaven because I'm a believer. John 3v16 does not say anything about repenting. Believing is all I have to do.'

'Once saved, always saved', you may say. 'Salvation is a gift, and cannot be taken away from anyone' some may say. 'As long as I believe in Jesus, I am saved.'

So, let's summarise and look at the different ways that people can think they are a Christian and will go to heaven.

Some believe Christianity is about a relationship with God. Others think that belonging to a church is proof that a person is a Christian. And there are those who think that 'belief' is enough. As long as you 'believe' Jesus died on the cross, then you are assured eternal life in heaven because of what John 3v16 says. Who is correct, and who could be wrong in their thinking?

Before we move on to the next chapter, let's briefly look at something else. How does a lady become a mother? She gets pregnant and will one day give birth to a baby. On the day she gives birth she is now a mother. She can tell all her friends she is a mother. Let's ask a few questions. Does the mother have to wash the baby? Or can the mother let the baby wear the same clothes for the first twelve months? Does the mother have to give the baby a comfortable place to sleep? Or can the mother leave the baby on the floor all day and night so that she saves money and does not have to buy a bed for the baby? She is still a mother regardless of how she looks after the baby, and even if the baby is not fed and dies after a few days, she can still tell all her friends that she was once a mother.

Do mothers want their babies to grow? Or are they just pleased simply to tell all their friends that they have given birth to a baby? What is a mothers joy? What gives her happiness and joy in her life? Just to know she has a baby? Or does she long for more? Would she like the baby to grow and start walking one day? What does the mother want?

She desires to see the baby grow. Parents want the best for their children. No one likes to see a child failing in their education or being bullied at school. Everyone delights in the best for their children. And God, our Father, desires to see us grow too. He has no intention of us remaining Christian babies all throughout our lives. Let us therefore look into the Word of God and see what God longs for in our lives.

Chapter 3 - The Word of God

Let's begin by looking at John 3v16. Let's look at the possibility that as long as we 'believe' in Jesus then we are saved. Nothing else matters. Repentance, forgiveness and hatred are irrelevant. As long as we 'believe' in Jesus then we are saved.

John 3v16 comes from the Word of God. The Bible has sixty six books, thirty nine in the Old Testament and twenty seven in the New Testament. The gospel of John is just one of those sixty six books. And the question is, "Are the other books relevant?"

If they are not relevant, then why do we have a Bible with an Old Testament and New Testament? What's the purpose of all the other stories in the Bible? Why do people rest on 25th December every year and spend a lot of money buying Christmas Cards and presents here in the UK? Why are banks and many other businesses shut every year on 25th December? What's the purpose of someone telling a story of two people, Mary and Joseph, who went to Bethlehem and had a little baby called Jesus? Why do people tell a story about a man called Noah who built an ark? What's the relevance of all these things? Why do so many churches across the whole wide world open their doors on 25th December for a church service? What's the point? If John 3v16 tells us how to get to heaven, then why do we need to know anything else?

One way to begin to answer this question is to get a Bible and begin to read it. What does it actually say? What is the purpose of the Bible? What is the message in the Word of God? Let us look at some of the many stories in the Bible.

God did not want the Israelites to remain in Egypt, so he raised up a leader who would take them into the promised land which was flowing with milk and honey – see Exodus 3v8.

We are stop to stop stealing and go and work for money – see Ephesians 4v28.

Hannah wanted a baby, and she was given a baby boy called Samuel – see 1 Samuel 1v20.

People were hungry, and there was enough food to feed over 5,000 people – see John 6v10-12.

All these are in the Bible. But you may be asking yourself, "What's the relevance? As long as I believe in Jesus, that is enough. Why do I need to hear so many stories from the Bible?"

Look at this story. People were living in hard times. Exodus 2v23-24 says:

"And it came to pass in process of time, that the king of Egypt died: and the children of Israel sighed by reason of the bondage, and they cried, and their cry came up unto God by reason of the bondage. And God heard their groaning, and God remembered his covenant with Abraham, with Isaac, and with Jacob."

They were groaning. They did not like the way they had to live. God wanted to help them, and so he made a way for them to move out of Egypt and prepared a promised land for them. God loved them and wanted to help them.

Look at all the other verses above. When someone decides to turn to God, the Bible tells them to stop living a bad life. No one likes it when someone steals something from them. We are told to stop stealing and to work. Now look at Hannah. She was very sad because her sister was a mother but she was not. She did not have her own child and she longed for one. She was very sad and cried. God heard her and promised her a child, and she had a baby boy. Now look at Jesus. He had a large crowd around him and they were hungry. It seemed as though there would not be enough food to feed all the people. But there was. Jesus took care of them and fed them all.

But were these things actually necessary? Did God really need to help the Israelites? Does a person really need to change their ways? Did God actually need to respond to the cries of Hannah's heart and give her a baby? Did Jesus really need to feed the crowd?

Is love necessary? Is kindness necessary? Do we really want people to live a righteous life in our community and stop stealing? What is the purpose of our daily life? Why do we wash our clothes? Why do we buy food? Why do we help others? What's the purpose? Do we need to love? Does a mother have to love her baby? What is our motive for all that we do? What is life all about if we want to be a Christian?

The Bible has many stories about situations that changed. There was once a big tall man waiting for others to come and fight him, and eventually David defeated him with a stone. There were a lot of people with no food and who had to travel to Egypt to buy corn, and Joseph enabled them all to have some corn. There was a lame man who asked for money, and one day he was told to get up and walk and he began walking. And there was a man who was very generous and helped others, but something was lacking in his own life and Peter went to his home and gave him the Holy Spirit. The Bible tells us again and again how things changed in people's lives.

Is change actually necessary in our world today? Think about life four hundred years ago when people were living in the 17th century. Look at the life of some of the richest people in the 17th century. How many people could wake up, turn on the computer and check their emails? No one. However rich a person was, there was no emailing in the 17th century. Computers did not exist. And no one could travel to an airport in London and fly to Hong Kong in a day. Airports did not exist in the 17th century. If people in the UK wanted to travel abroad they would go on a ship. And if people wanted to contact a family member who was living some twenty miles away, they would write a letter and send it to them in the post. Instant communication through emails and text messages on mobile phones simply did not exist four hundred years ago.

Why did the world need to change? Why did people need to invent computers, mobile phones and aeroplanes? If others lived without them for so many centuries, then why do we need them now? The simple answer is that people looked for ways to improve our society.

If someone can travel from London to Glasgow in one hour by plane, then why spend seven or eight hours travelling by car or train? Flying is much quicker, so why use a slower means of transport? Someone can go to an airport in London at 8am, leave at 10.00am for Glasgow and be in a meeting in Glasgow by 12pm. The meeting can finish at 3pm and they return to the airport and are back in London by 8pm. How many people can leave London at 9am, drive to Glasgow, have a meeting and be back in London by 8pm? Aeroplanes are a lot faster and save a lot of time, and enable someone to accomplish much more in a day.

So are we glad that people are creative and full of ideas and invent things such as computers, mobile phones and aeroplanes? Are we glad a home can have a fridge and we can preserve things such as milk and yoghurts? Are we pleased, or should we get rid of all these things and go back to living like people did in the 17th century? Let's look again at the 17th century.

There were no cars. No one had to pay for car tax or car insurance. There were no mobile phones. No one had to look for a place to charge their mobile phones. There were no airports. People could not go to work at an airport in the 17th century simply because there were no airports. The aeroplane had not been invented at that time.

The question therefore is, do we like a changing world, or do we wish everything would always remain the same? Think about everything remaining the same in the world all the time. There are no new products. There are no new roads or houses. Everything remains the same. And the gospel just remains one simple verse – John 3v16. "Everyone who *believes* ... eternal life." Forget about love, forget about forgiveness and repentance. Forget about fellowship and service. Just believe. Just look at this one verse and forget the rest of the Bible.

What's the relevance of Psalm 23? It says in verse two, "He leads me beside still waters." 'What's the point?' you may say. 'I like my home in the town, so why do I need to go for a walk and be beside still waters?' What's the relevance of the parable of the lost sheep? If I choose to care for a sheep, that's my personal decision. Why should I care for a sheep if I don't want to? I have a choice in my life. So why do we need to hear such a parable? What is the relevance? Surely I can just work, earn money, die and go to heaven because I'm a believer. Are other things in life actually relevant or necessary? Do we really need cars? Do we really need mobile phones? Or are they unnecessary?

Are we wasting time buying good food to eat on Christmas Day? Why do we spend time going to a funeral or burial just because someone has died? They're gone, so forget about it. What's the point of mourning? And why get excited when a lady gives birth to a baby? It's just another person here on earth. What's the point of joy and laughter, or weeping and mourning? What is the purpose of all these things?

Or do we get great joy when someone has a very beautiful baby? Do we get so richly blessed when a couple are having a wedding? Are we thrilled when a child completes their studies and has a graduation ceremony? Why do we think and act like we do?

I think about my own life. I was very blessed one day when my son got his A Level results. Within a couple of months he was about to go and begin his university degree. My wife and I were so pleased for him. We were blessed when he got his university accommodation and were happy to take him there and help him as he settled into his new place of residence, about to begin his degree.

And it was also a great joy when he completed his degree. He did very well and it was a delight to go along to his graduation ceremony. He worked hard and did so well in his studies. My wife and I were so pleased for him.

This brings me back to the question about the Word of God. Why should I read the Bible? What's the purpose and relevance of the Bible? Is there any benefit in the Bible, and if so, what are the benefits? I believe there is much. The truth is, everyone is blessed by changes in our world. Parents are blessed when their child starts school and has a good education, and again they are blessed when a child completes their education and gets a good job. Others are pleased when someone has their first grandchild. People delight in others.

"Doesn't your son work so hard? He really does a good job in the office."

"Look at the way she dresses so smartly in the office. She looks to lovely."

We enjoy praising others and affirming how wonderful people are doing. Life could be very dull if we just ate the same food all the time and always wore the same clothes. We never dress smartly for a wedding or a graduation but always wear the same clothes wherever we go. Life could be very dull. And yet we all love variety in life. This is very evident by the fact that we can take several minutes in a supermarket just to decide what food to buy. There are many choices and we enjoy eating different things. "Shall I buy chocolate ice cream for the children or strawberry ice cream? Or shall I buy a trifle for a change? What shall I get for the family to enjoy?" We all enjoy a variety of things in our lives.

The Bible is such a good book to read because it shows how situations can be changed. God is there to help us. He wants to bless us. The Bible contains testimonies of those who prayed and their prayers were answered, and those who prayed and fasted and God did things. Here are just a few examples.

And Jabez called on the God of Israel saying, "Oh, that You would bless me indeed, and enlarge my territory, that Your hand would be with me, and that You would keep *me* from evil, that I may not cause pain!" So God granted him what he requested. 1 Chronicles 4v10

Then the secret was revealed to Daniel in a night vision. So Daniel blessed the God of heaven. Daniel 2v19

Peter was therefore kept in prison, but constant prayer was offered to God for him by the church. And when Herod was about to bring him out, that night Peter was sleeping, bound with two chains between two soldiers; and the guards before the door were keeping the prison. Now behold, an angel of the Lord stood by *him,* and a light shone in the prison; and he struck Peter on the side and raised him up, saying, "Arise quickly!" And his chains fell off *his* hands. Acts 12v5-7

As they ministered to the Lord and fasted, the Holy Spirit said, "Now separate to Me Barnabas and Saul for the work to which I have called them." Then, having fasted and prayed, and laid hands on them, they sent *them* away. Acts 13v2-3

And so we need to ask a question. If a person simply 'believes' in God and they never read their Bible or go to church, then is there something they could be missing in their lives? What about if they just go to church and show commitment to the church? Is that sufficient to ensure they go to heaven? Do they actually have to read their Bible in their home every day, or can they just be content to go to church and hear the minister preach a message every Sunday? The truth is, there is a lot in the Bible for us all to know, and I want to share a number of things with you so that your life may be richly blessed. Let us start by looking at our life in heaven. In the next chapter we will look at eternal treasures.

Chapter 4 – Eternal Treasures

The Bible talks about two places, heaven and hell. Matthew 25v46 talks about everlasting punishment and eternal life. No one wants to go to hell. That is a fact. The description of hell in Luke 16v23-24 is too unbearable, and everyone wants to enter heaven when they die. Yes, it would be great for everyone to go to heaven.

Heaven is beautiful. It is a very wonderful place. However, when I read the Bible, I do not believe that life in heaven will be the same for every single person who goes to heaven. Let us look at these two verses:

"If any man's work abide which he hath built thereupon, he shall receive a reward. If any man's work shall be burned, he shall suffer loss: but he himself shall be saved; yet so as by fire." 1 Corinthians 3v14-15

The Bible says that if any man's work shall be burned, he shall suffer loss, but he himself shall be saved. This is saying that a person can be saved and go to heaven and yet suffer loss. You may ask yourself, "How can anyone suffer in heaven?"

The Bible says that a person will suffer loss. That means they simply cannot be rewarded as verse 14 says. And the easiest way to describe this is with a picture. Three families were all going for a walk along the beach. They noticed a lot of litter on the beach and two families decided to help to clear up the litter. Later the town clerk came and saw how beautiful the beach was and decided to buy some chicken and chips for the two families who had helped to clear up all the litter. One family just sat on the beach and did nothing whilst the others enjoyed their chicken and chips. Two families enjoyed a reward, but the other family had nothing to enjoy. They suffered loss.

No one hurt the other family or stole their possessions. No one shouted at them or bullied them in any way. They were safe and in good health. So some could argue and say that they were not suffering in any way on the beach. However, they were simply unable to eat any chicken and chips. In that context, they suffered loss. They were not in pain in any way, and in heaven there will be no pain (bullying or injuries) as Revelation 21v4 says. But people may suffer loss.

What do we want in heaven? Eternal rewards all the time, or nothing? Do we want to be rewarded, or are we quite happy just to have a healthy body that can go for a walk all the time? Let's look back to life in the 17th century once again. Would we be happy today, in the 21st century, to write letters all the time and never use digital communication? Would we be happy to walk everywhere and never use a car or motorbike to travel to places? If people walked many places in the 17th century, surely we too can do so in the 21st century? Do we really need cars, buses and taxis? Are they actually necessary?

The truth is, they provide very many benefits. If we want to go to the supermarket and buy lots of food, the bags of shopping can be very heavy to carry when we walk along the road. But if we have a car and can drive to the supermarket, we can buy our food, put it in the car and drive to our home, take the shopping out of the car and straight into the house. And if it is raining, we will not get soaked like those who have to walk because we remain dry when we are in the car. Vehicles are very useful and can benefit us in many ways.

Who, in the 17th century, could ever imagine that someone could take a photo of a new born baby in Australia and show it to a friend in the UK in less than thirty minutes? "It's impossible to send a photo all that distance in thirty minutes. No bird, no ship or person can ever get a photo delivered that far in thirty minutes. It's absolutely impossible," some may say.

What about at the beginning of the 20th century when aeroplanes were around? Could someone send a wedding photo from East Africa to the UK in thirty minutes? Can an aeroplane fly from Nairobi in Kenya to London in the UK in thirty minutes? Impossible. It cannot be done. And yet today, in the 21st century, I can attend a wedding in East Africa, take a photo, attach it to an email and send it to my family back in the UK and it is with them within less than thirty minutes. The world has changed in many ways in the last one hundred years.

How many blessings do we want to enjoy in heaven for all eternity? Or do we really not care and are quite glad just to enter heaven and suffer loss and escape the fire of hell? Have we ever really given thought to what life would be like for all eternity in heaven? Or do we just look at the Bible and believe in heaven and hell and think nothing more about life after death? Heaven is a place we should be seriously thinking about.

I shared earlier on about a lady having a baby and becoming a mother. Many years go by and the child is now 18 years old and has just finished their secondary education. The teenager has a choice, to get work as a window cleaner and earn money cleaning the windows of some local homes, or to go to university and get a degree and become a teacher. A window cleaner may earn $5 a day but a school teacher may earn $40 a day. Which is better, to study at university and become a teacher or to finish education immediately and start earning money as soon as possible? It's good to think about the future, especially our eternal life.

The Bible says this in Hebrews 11v24-26:

"By faith Moses, when he became of age, refused to be called the son of Pharaoh's daughter, choosing rather to suffer affliction with the people of God than to enjoy the passing pleasures of sin, esteeming the reproach of Christ greater riches than the treasures in Egypt; for he looked to the reward." NKJV

Verse 26 says he was looking ahead to his reward. Moses was thinking about his reward in heaven instead of his life on earth. But just how long is our life in heaven?

A '1' with two zeros is a hundred. A '1' with three zeros is a thousand. A '1' with six zeros is a million. What is a '1' with thirty zeros? What is a '1' with fifty zeros?

I write down 1,000,000. This is one million. Can you imagine living in heaven for one million years? What about a 'one' with a forty zeros? Can you imagine living in heaven for 10,000,000,000,000,000,000,000,000,000,000,000,000,000 years?

Try to imagine what it is like living forever and ever and ever. Once someone enters heaven, there is no turning back and going back to earth. What God gives a person on judgment day is theirs forever. If he gives you something every day, it is yours forever and ever in heaven. No one can take it away from you. If you are not given any eternal reward, there is nothing you can do. You will be in heaven but suffer loss forever and ever.

You can never return to earth and have a second chance to do God's work. Imagine every day you are sitting on the beach with the other families. There they are, every single day, enjoying their chicken and chips and you are not. You are suffering loss.

Now let's look at life as a parent. A child is at university. They phone home to tell their parents they have no money for food and are very hungry. They have not eaten for the last few days. The parents can decide to send them money. Do you want your child to spend the money on a new car or alcohol and then complain that they still have no money for food? Or do you want your child to eat good food and have a very healthy life for many years? Parents long for the best in their child's life, and God longs for the best in our lives too.

God is a Father. The first two words of the Lord's prayer are "Our Father" and this tells us that we are a child of God. As our Father, God wants us to enjoy very many things in our lives and has a lot to give us. But a child cannot receive things later on in life unless they are prepared to work for them. And God promises to reward us, for all eternity, when we serve Him with all our heart and do the things He asks us to do. If we decline, then we cannot be rewarded.

I go back to my earlier example of the three families on the beach. I cannot demand that the other two families share their chicken and chips with me at all. I have to let them enjoy their rewards and must not steal any of the food from them. I admit that the other families did ask me if I would be willing to help them clear up all the litter but I just decided to be lazy and sit and enjoy the beach. Now I'm not able to enjoy the chicken and chips because I was not rewarded by the Town Clerk. I have to accept the consequences of my decision.

Would we like God to give us such beautiful, abundant eternal treasures for all eternity? Jesus tells us to store up treasures in heaven (Matthew 6v20), and wants every one of us to receive many treasures for all eternity. Perhaps we need to give time to really think about our life in heaven. Let us use our imagination and look at these pictures of three people in heaven.

One person gets 5$ a day. At the end of the day his money is gone. The next day he gets another 5$. He can never save up. As a result, he cannot ever travel more than five miles from his home. He is not able to see the beautiful mountains in the other places and the lovely flowers in the fields a hundred miles away. He is suffering loss because he received a very small reward.

Another person gets 50$ a day. They are always enjoying the creation in many places. They love the trees in some forests, the waters in other places and the many mountains and hills in so many places. They really enjoy all the creation and are so blessed to see so many places.

Another person gets 200$ a day. The huge choices of places to enjoy and all the fruit juices are just so wonderful. Glasses of mango juice, apple juice, strawberry juice and pineapple juice are just so lovely. They have endless opportunities to enjoy unlimited glasses of fruit juices in heaven. "I could never imagine there would be such beautiful juices in heaven and so many lovely places to see. This is beyond words", says the person.

One person is in heaven glad to be there for all eternity, but unable to experience the beautiful mountains and hills around them. Another is glad to travel and see many places, and has endless glasses of water to drink all the time in heaven. They are never thirsty. Never.

But the third person really cannot describe the rich, beautiful blessings they received from God on judgment day. They never imagined God would give them so much. They are full of so much joy and delight in heaven.

Would we like to be rewarded for all eternity? If so, how do we get rewarded? What is God looking for from our lives?

From this chapter, we can see that life has many choices. We can choose what to do with our lives. There are so many good things we can enjoy in our lives today, such as mobile phones and aeroplanes. We have a lot to enjoy here on earth. Like a child who chooses to finish their secondary education and go on to university to get a degree and a good job, so we could begin to think about how we can get a good reward once we leave earth and enter heaven.

Let's therefore look into the Word of God and look at the Christian life. We can discover why the Word of God is such a beautiful book to read.

Chapter 5 – The Heart

As I think back to life as a teenager, I reflect on some of the worship songs I would sing in church.

"Soften my heart, Lord. Soften my heart. From all indifference, set me apart."

"Open the eyes of my heart Lord. Open the eyes of my heart."

"Blaze, spirit blaze. Set our hearts on fire."

All these songs would refer to the heart. The question is 'why'? As long as we believe in Jesus, attend church and act in a polite way all the time, everyone around us can see that we are a committed

Christian. What's the heart got to do with Christian service? We simply do our duty and help with church events when needed so that we are all helping with everything. Churches cannot afford to pay everyone all the time and they rely a lot on volunteers, so if we want to keep the church going then we have to be willing to all serve and help with church activities. We just get on and do things so that the church can carry out all the activities in the building.

If you go to a shop to buy something for 1US$ and give a 20 US$ note, you expect 19 US$ in return. The cashier does not take the money and say 'goodbye' to you. They give you the change. They are not doing this from their heart because they love you as a personal friend, but simply because it is their duty. Every cashier does this so that people are treated fairly. They simply do their job.

People can look at the Christian life in the same way. But when one reads the Bible, we find many scriptures that refer to the heart. In the book of 1 Samuel we read this:

"But the Lord said to Samuel, "Do not look at his appearance or at his physical stature, because I have refused him. For the Lord does not see as man sees; for man looks at the outward appearance, but the Lord looks at *the heart*." 1 Samuel 16v7 - NKJV

What does the Bible say about the heart? Let me share two pictures with you.

Hard heart   Soft heart

When a heart is soft, the Lord can begin to prune the heart and make it ready to bear more fruit as John 15v2 says. A hard heart can be set in fixed ways and very difficult to change.

Psalm 95v7-8 says, "If you hear his voice, do not harden your heart." A person with a hard heart can refuse to obey God. They do not want to change. Their heart is hardened.

And in the gospel of Mark, we read:

"For they had not understood about the loaves, because their heart was hardened." Mark 6v52 NKJV

This verse also says that the hearts of the disciples were hardened. Now let's look at another verse.

"Then the family heads of Judah and Benjamin, and the priests and Levites—everyone whose heart God had moved—prepared to go up and build the house of the Lord in Jerusalem." Ezra 1v5 NIV

This verse talks about everyone whose heart God had moved. A soft heart is a heart willing to change for God.

Let's give an illustration about a hard heart and a soft heart.

A group of people had been in a church for several years and built up very good relationships with each other. Every Sunday they would bring food and eat together after the church service. A new person joined the church and had a lovely heart. The Holy Spirit said to the group, "Invite this person to join you for lunch and let them become part of the group. They have a lot to share."

A hard-hearted person may think, "I've built up a very good relationship with these people and do not want the unity to be destroyed or ruined in any way. Let me keep things the way they are. I'll not let anyone else join us in case they spoil the beauty in the group. And also, it will cost us more money, as we will have to buy food for another person. Let us tell them to stay away."

A kind-hearted person with a soft heart could think, "I would like to welcome this person to join us every Sunday for lunch and get to know us more. Let me invite them to come with us for lunch."

There is a difference between a person with a hard heart and one with a soft heart. One blesses God in a very wonderful way when a person is made welcome and is able to join a group of people, but the other is lacking in love.

Now look at judgment day. 1 Corinthians 3v14 says each person's work will be tested by fire. Would God want to remember the person for all eternity who, because of the rich unity already in the group, did not want to invite the new person along? Or will God prefer to forget about this matter and burn it up? Will God want to forget about the kind-hearted people who made the person so welcome, or will he choose to remember their kindness and love? The Bible says that God will not forget the love you have shown – Hebrews 6v10. So, every time we show love and give the glory and honour to God, he will be blessed and remember our deeds for all eternity. But if we decline to show love, is there any point in remembering the event? It is better just to burn it up so that it is gone forever. Who wants to remember events for all eternity that were done with no love? 'Without love, we are nothing' says the Bible in 1 Corinthians 13v3.

God sees everything we do. He knows everything – 1 John 3v19, and nothing is hidden from Him as Luke 12v2-3 says. He knows all our thoughts as Psalm 139v2 says. God wants us to have 'lovely' thoughts as Philippians 4v8 says. How much of our thoughts, words and deeds are a blessing to God and will give us a wonderful eternal reward in heaven and how much will be burnt up on judgment day?

Look at this scripture and look at two people's reactions.

2 Corinthians 9v7 says, "Every man according as he purposed in his heart, so let him give; not grudgingly, or of necessity: for God loveth a cheerful giver." NKJV.

People are asked to give a gift to a family that has just moved into the village. One person gladly gives some cash because they don't want the family to starve and go without food. Another family reluctantly gives some cash, but feels that the family should look for a job and earn their own cash instead of expecting handouts all the time. One gives cheerfully and God will remember such a beautiful, loving deed for all eternity. Another gives reluctantly because they don't want to be known as the stingy family in the community and feel they ought to give to prove they are not being selfish. Will God remember such a deed done with a reluctant spirit, or will God be eternally thankful for their gift? God loves a cheerful giver, so a cheerful person who gives generously will always be a blessing to God, but what about one who gives but with a reluctant heart? Our thoughts could make a difference between whether we are rewarded abundantly in heaven or could suffer loss for all eternity. God wants us to have lovely thoughts all the time as Philippians 4v8 says. One thing we can be completely sure of is that a lovely thought is always a blessing to God, especially when it is accompanied by a lovely deed.

But even then, do our thoughts lead to deeds? We can think about many good deeds but fail to turn them into action. We can have a lot of good motives but fail to do anything. Our seeds fall onto the footpath and the birds come and eat them up as the parable of the sower says. Good thoughts need to be turned into good deeds. 1 John 3v18 tells us not to love only with words but also with action.

In chapter 3 there were two questions. 'Why should I read the Bible? What's the purpose and relevance of the Bible?' I trust by now we are starting to see the richness of the Word of God. It is an absolutely beautiful book. The Bible gives us promises and assurances that we will not find anywhere else. It gives us hope and blessings that simply cannot be got from any other source. And it offers us wonderful eternal treasures when we serve the Lord with all our heart. It is an absolutely wonderful book.

Let's look once again at a husband and a wife. A wife says to her husband that she would like to buy some new curtains for the bedroom, and asks him if he is willing to replace the curtains. He can decline and say that he would prefer not to spend money on new curtains but instead save the money to get a new car in the next few years, or he can be 100% pleased and very glad to fit the new curtains. He can turn down the request, or he can be delighted with the request from his wife and go ahead with what she wants.

How does a wife feel when a husband responds with a delightful heart? Of course she is pleased. When a husband declines, she has to accept his decision. She still loves him and knows he loves her, but is not always able to enjoy the things in the home that she would like. She learns to accept his decision. There is nothing wrong with his decision, but his priority is the car whereas her first priority is the home.

The husband is not against his wife, but choosing to put his priority in another place. He is not being unloving like the husband who always had the radio on every night at full volume. He simply believes the car should take priority in the family finances.

When we put God first, is He not also delighted with us? Of course he is. We can be asked to fast and pray for an event. We can respond with delight, or choose to decline. Another time a person can seek some time with a companion to talk about some matters, and we can either give them time or decline. God can be blessed with our lives and increase our treasures in heaven when we do the things He asks us to do, or he can accept our decision to decline.

If we read the Bible every day, we can become full of peace and joy, and confident in God every time we pray and do what He asks us to do. Our relationship with God can get richer and more intimate. We can all look forward to a very beautiful eternal life in heaven, because God is blessed with all the love and kindness he sees in our hearts and our deeds all done as a result of all the wonderful love in our hearts. Knowing all this, what is the role of the church?

When we get saved, people often suggest that we join a church in order to grow. We can decide to regularly attend a church and show much loyalty to the church. But is that it? Do we simply serve in the church until we die? Or is there more?

What is the church's role? We will look at this in the next chapter.

Chapter 6 –
The Church

The church is a body as 1 Corinthians 12v27 says. And the church has leaders.

Ephesians 4v11 says that God "gave some, apostles; and some, prophets; and some, evangelists; and some, pastors and teachers."

Verse 12 says:

"To equip his people for works of service, so that the body of Christ may be built up." Ephesians 4v12 - NIV

The leaders in our churches referred to in verse 11 are there (1) to equip us all for works of service and (2) to build us all up (verse 12). This would imply that we do not remain babies all our lives in the kingdom of God but that we are being built up and equipped to serve. This is the role of the church.

But is this being achieved? Or is the church simply wanting everyone to remain in the same place all the time, keeping the people where they are, so that things do not change and everything is carried out in the same way all the time? Has the church become set in the way it does things so that it does not think about the growth of its people?

If a person becomes a Christian and joins a church, they can be encouraged to know that every time they serve the Lord and bless Him with deeds done from a heart of love, they are storing up treasures in heaven. Their deeds are not done in vain or unnoticed, but every time they show love they are a rich blessing to God and God will not forget the love they are showing. They can be built up to know that they will have a very rich reward in heaven for all eternity as they choose to serve God and honour Him in their lives every day.

If someone does not know this, then they can allow bitterness and envy to enter their heart. "Why is it that four people all became Christians last year, but two of us always help with the church cleaning whilst the other two come to the church and do nothing except sit through the church service every Sunday? Surely everyone should serve and not just the two of us." It's possible to feel bitter because only two people are serving instead of four.

But when one knows that their service for God, done out of a heart of love, is going to give them eternal treasures in heaven, then they no longer feel bitter but instead seek to encourage others not to be lazy but to also look at ways to serve God and also store up treasures in heaven. Ones' heart simply longs for others also to have a rich, eternal life. Teaching the Word and building others up is very important so that there is no envy or jealousy in the church but a lot of love and encouragement for others in the church family. We continually encourage others to serve God and honour Him from a heart full of love for God, knowing what a delight we are to God.

Without such knowledge, it's so easy to have the same thoughts as Martha. Look at this verse.

But Martha was distracted with much serving, and she approached Him and said, "Lord, do you not care that my sister has left me to serve alone? Therefore tell her to help me." Luke 10v40 NKJV

Martha wondered why she was left to do all the work by herself. It can seem very unfair. But when one looks at everything from an eternal perspective, such a person can live with joy and delight in their heart knowing that one day, God will reward them for all eternity. Service is a continual joy, knowing that God rewards everyone for all their deeds as Psalm 62v12 says.

Let's also look at the older brother in the parable of the prodigal son. Look at Luke 15:

"The older brother became angry and refused to go in. So his father went out and pleaded with him. But he answered his father, 'Look! All these years I've been slaving for you and never disobeyed your orders. Yet you never gave me even a young goat so I could celebrate with my friends. But when this son of yours who has squandered your property with prostitutes comes home, you kill the fattened calf for him!' Luke 15v28-30 - NIV

The older brother felt forgotten by the Father. He did a lot of hard work and the father never even gave him a goat to celebrate with his friends as verse 29 says. He was focussing on his earthly rewards and not thinking about his eternal rewards. But listen to what the Father says in verse 31.

'My son,' the father said, 'you are always with me, and everything I have is yours.' Luke 15v31 NIV

The older brother would inherit everything when the Father died. 'Everything I have is yours' said the Father to the older brother. Everything. His hard work was not ever in vain but would one day be rewarded when he gets to inherit all his father's property.

So, we go to a church to be built up as Ephesians 4v12 says and also to be equipped for service. But let's look more at the church.

There was a time when a UK charity held an event in London about international aid. In 2011, Tear Fund held an event called "Tea Time for Change" and invited the Secretary of State for International Development, Andrew Mitchell MP, along to the event. Andrew spoke at the event, and one of the things he said was that 'aid should be a means to an end, and not an end in itself.'

What he was saying was that foreign aid is given to third world countries to enable them to end their poverty and start to become self-reliant, but it is possible for people to think of aid as an end in itself. Nations can prepare their annual financial budget and build in foreign aid simply as another source of income to meet all their ongoing expenses every year. Aid is not looked at as a means of ending poverty but rather as a source of income to help meet the annual expenses of the government's budget.

Could it be that the church is not looked at any longer as a means of equipping the body for God's work, but instead the church is looked at as an end in itself? The purpose of church no longer becomes a place of equipping the people for works of service and building them up, but instead becomes focussed on the finances and the maintenance of the building. The content of the Word of God is no longer the priority of the church. Instead the priority is to ensure there is enough income to keep the place functioning throughout the year and ensure that all the expenses can be met. Has the church no longer got its focus on the Word of God and instead turned its focus to its own needs?

How do churches even get leaders? In the UK there are Bible colleges, and if a person wants to become a church minister, then they can be encouraged to study with a Bible college for a period of time. Once they complete their studies, they can see which churches have a vacancy for a minister and consider applying for a position with a church. Churches can advertise for a minister in a Christian newspaper or magazine and look for a person to take over the leadership of the church once the previous minister has left the church.

Could it be that leading a church is seen to be simply a way of earning a salary? Everyone needs to work, whether they are a school teacher, a supermarket manager, a cashier in a bank or a church minister, and everyone wants a salary. And the Bible says in 1 Corinthians 9v14:

"In the same way, the Lord has commanded that those who preach the gospel should receive their living from the gospel." NIV

Has the focus for church leaders simply become their job requirements and their own life rather than the growth of the people in the church? Is the leader only concerned about having enough money in the church for their regular salary and ensuring that they do the work they are required to do as the minister, and not concerned for the growth of the people?

If a leader were fully devoted to the growth of their people, they would ask regular questions. A baby does not remain a baby after five years. It becomes a child and is expected to go to school. How long does someone continue to sit and receive teachings on a

Sunday? For five years? Or twenty five years? Or should they reach a point when they too should start to teach others what they are learning?

Another role for the church is to help us all live clean and pure lives. A very important question we need to ask ourselves is this. "Is repentance necessary in our lives if we want to go to heaven?" Jesus said in the gospel of Mark to repent.

"And saying, the time is fulfilled, and the kingdom of God is at hand: repent ye, and believe the gospel." Mark 1v15

Do we believe we have to repent in order to go to heaven, or is it sufficient just to believe that Jesus died for us, that is, that the Good Friday story is true, and therefore we can live an unclean life? If we do have to repent, how many sins must we repent of? Some sins, most sins, or all of our sins?

Look at how God sees our sins in James 2v10:

"For whosoever shall keep the whole law, and yet offend in one point, he is guilty of all."

Even one sin is bad in God's eyes. God wants us to repent of every sin and not just a majority of sins. He looks for hearts that are completely pure and not just mostly pure. There is a difference between a car that is completely clean and a car where the majority is clean but just a small bit of dirt on the front window. And God sees whether our hearts are completely clean or not. He sees where we are unclean and not repenting of sins.

If that is so and God wants us to be completely clean, then we have to read the Bible in order to know what God likes and what He dislikes. Let me share two verses.

"If anyone, then, knows the good they ought to do and doesn't do it, it is sin for them." James 4v17 NIV

"For when for the time ye ought to be teachers, ye have need that one teach you again which be the first principles of the oracles of God." Hebrews 5v12

Notice the word 'ought'. In James 4v17 we read that we are sinning when we do not do the things we ought to do. So we should make a note of this and ask ourselves what things we ought to do for God and see if we are actually doing them. Then, when we read the Bible, we can read the word 'ought' again as we do in Hebrews 5v12. One of the things we ought to do is to 'teach others.' The Bible says that by this time we ought to be teachers. Could this be a sin in our lives, when we are not teaching others but instead continually going to church and expecting to be taught by someone else all the time? Could this be one area in our lives that God does not like, and in His eyes we are no different to someone breaking the whole law?

We can all say we are saved by grace though faith – Ephesians 2v8. But what else do we read about the grace of God? Look at Titus 2:

"For the grace of God has appeared that offers salvation to all people. It teaches us to say "no" to ungodliness and worldly passions, and to live self-controlled, upright and godly lives in this present age." Titus 2v11-12 NIV

We should say 'no' to ungodliness. If we refuse to repent and choose to live an ungodly life, are we actually following God? In Jude we see that the word 'ungodly' is repeated. Could this be one of the ungodly things God is not pleased with in our lives, our refusal to teach the Word of God to others? Have we instead chosen a lifestyle of just sitting in church and receiving Sunday after Sunday? Are we ever going to start to teach others? How many times does the world 'ungodly' get mentioned in these verses?

Now Enoch, the seventh from Adam, prophesied about these men also, saying, "Behold, the Lord comes with ten thousands of His saints, to execute judgment on all, to convict all who are *ungodly* among them of all their *ungodly* deeds which they have committed in an *ungodly* way, and of all the harsh things which *ungodly* sinners have spoken against Him." Jude v 14-15 NKJV

Four times we see the word 'ungodly' mentioned. God wants us to get rid of our ungodly ways. So if we have to repent, are church leaders ensuring that we obey the Word of God and become clean in every area of our lives? Or are our church leaders more concerned about keeping the congregation at peace and satisfied so that funds continue to flow regularly into the church and the minister can be paid every month?

Like a UK university, people join every year and people graduate and leave every year. There is a constant flow of students joining universities and also graduating and moving on every year. Should there not also be a constant flow of new people entering our churches and people leaving to start teaching others?

Let's go back to the church and the Word of God. The Bible says that the foundation of the church is Apostles and Prophets – Ephesians 2v20. And Apostles are the most important anointing in the church as 1 Corinthians 12v28 says. Let's look at this verse.

"And God hath set some in the church, first apostles, secondarily prophets, thirdly teachers, after that miracles, then gifts of healings, helps, governments, diversities of tongues." 1 Corinthians 12v28 NKJV

Administrators are not the most important people in the church. Apostles are. Administrators will want to make sure that all the expenses can be met from the regular income that the church is getting, but Apostles look at the work that God has called the church to do and decide to step out in faith. How many churches prefer to put administration as the greatest priority in the church and reject the apostolic anointing? In Chapter 14 we will look at Apostles and Prophets in the church.

Are churches actually operating according to the whole of the Word of God, or simply doing a few good things in order to look like a good Christian place to join? A church can have a few songs for a time of worship, a sermon, prayers and an offering so that it does what other churches do and looks like a good place to be part of. It just gets on with the things that look traditional inside a church.

Remember, the church is there to equip God's people for works of service. Every church leader should want the very best for their flock and delight to see them getting very many eternal rewards in heaven. Naturally a parent delights to see a child do well in their education and get a good job, and a church leader should be pleased when the people are serving God wholeheartedly and doing everything the Holy Spirit says. What, therefore, is a good and healthy way to lead a church?

Let's begin by imagining some adults all book a place on an expedition for one week. One adult takes 1,000$, another 200$ and the other 50$. They all go separately to the shops and buy their food to cook on the expedition. One decides to buy bread and margarine and makes toast all the time. The other buys meat and vegetables and cooks a very healthy meal for himself. The third friend goes out for a walk and enters a local restaurant where he orders a beautifully cooked meal together with a drink.

We may be the person eating toast all the time. We are not hungry and we are not starving. But when our friend talks about the beautiful choices of drinks available in the local restaurant, do we feel pleased for him or do we envy him? Would we like the opportunity to join him one day in the restaurant? If he asks us to clean his car for him and says, in return, he will treat us to a free meal in the restaurant, do we take up the opportunity to clean his car for him or decline? We are not forced to do anything for him at all, and he is not forced to invite us to the restaurant. No one is forced to do anything for anyone. We can all choose to do whatever we wish. But we have to ask ourselves a question. Are we missing out on blessings because we do not want to serve and be a blessing to others? Could we be missing out on many things for all eternity in heaven because we declined many times to serve God and do things for Him?

How, therefore, can one lead a church in a good and healthy way? The most blessed way is to continually encourage everyone to have a deeper relationship with God. We want everyone to enjoy many wonderful treasures for all eternity. Any yet, to lead a church in such a way may sound very fearful and a big risk for a minister. What if everyone is so blessed to read the Bible that they all decide to go and teach others every Sunday and the church becomes empty? Suddenly there will be no one to bring money on a Sunday and the minister would be out of a job. It's better, therefore, to keep the church the way it is. It ensures there is a job for the minister.

But we must never forget God's promises. How does Luke 6v38 apply to the church and the minister? God could send new converts into the church and they begin to support the church financially as others are released. This verse says, "Give, and it shall be given to you." The question is, 'Do we believe?' Could it be that we living in a generation where we want to be sure of everything, including the church income, and we have reached a point where we will only live by sight and not by faith? We have to be sure things will work out so we choose a way that is comfortable to us; a way that ensures we will always have sufficient funds to keep the work going. Yet the Bible says "we live by faith, not by sight" in 2 Corinthians 5v7 and "what is not of faith is sin" in Romans 14v23. Do we even think of sin when we choose to live by sight and not by faith? Or do we think in a way that seems pleasing to those around us, regardless of how God feels about our choices?

To lead a church in a way that is always pleasing to God is to build up others all the time with a view to releasing them into ministry and having both the faith and the confidence that God will always send others into the church so that they too can be built up. Try to imagine a University lecturer always hoping that his students will fail every exam so that they remain in the university for another year and he is certain to remain in a job. No one would be pleased if students always failed their tests. Is God pleased if people remain in one church for a long period of time and are never released into ministry? Equipping everyone in the church to grow and to be released to teach others will please God in a very wonderful way, and God will always stand on His promises and send more people into the church. God is a covenant keeping God whose promises cannot fail. We have to believe this and hold onto Gods promises all the time and be always ready to act on them.

Let's now look at a couple of illustrations.

The first illustration is of a mother with a six month old baby. Let's imagine she prays that the baby never grows. "Please Lord, keep my six month old baby this size. I do not want to keep going to the shops to buy new clothes and new shoes. Please keep my baby the same size. Amen."

By not growing, one can save money. A Mum does not have to go and buy bigger shoes for the child. But can you imagine any mother wanting their child remain the same size forever and ever? Suppose my own mum had prayed this when I was six months old and I could not write at all in my life. Would I be able to write this book right now and share everything with you?

I believe every mother delights to see their child grow. Everyone is blessed to see their child growing and progressing in life. And that should be the heart of every church leader, to see all the people growing in their relationship with God.

The second illustration is about my hosts. I decide to go away to a mission and evangelise. I travel a long way and I stay with a host family for a week. I am not allowed to go and buy lots of alcohol and invite people into the home at 7pm for lots of drinks. My hosts may want a time of family devotions or to do other things, and will not want all my friends to be in their home. I have to respect the hosts and honour them. I cannot invite a lot of people in for a drink unless I ask them in advance.

My hosts may say that they like the home to be quiet so that their children can do their homework. My friends could be very noisy and that would make it very difficult for the children to do their work. I can go out to meet my friends but I cannot invite them into someone else's home. I have to respect my hosts.

I could argue and say that I've come here to serve, so I demand my hosts to let me have my own way. My willingness to serve does not give me authority to tell my hosts how to love me and give me what I want all the time. My hosts could ask me to leave on the basis that I'm making the place too noisy when my friends all enter and enjoy their alcohol. I have to remember that this is not my home, and if I am asked to leave then I could end up with nowhere to sleep. Look at this verse:

"Know ye not that your body is the temple of the Holy Ghost which is in you, which ye have of God, and ye are not your own? For ye are bought with a price: therefore glorify God in your body, and in your spirit, which are God's." 1 Corinthians 6v19-20

Do I own my life? No. God bought it – 1 Corinthians 6v19-20. Am I therefore allowed to ask God to give me what I want, all the time, or are there times when I am failing to respect him and honour him? I am in His kingdom so I respect Him. God is our Father, and just like any mother, he wants his children to grow. If I refuse to repent and regularly invite my friends in to my hosts house for some alcohol, will my hosts be happy? No. And is God happy if I refuse to repent and do not do the things I ought to do? No.

I could become very intellectual. I could say to my hosts, "Let me invite my friends in and have some alcohol. Respect me, and one day I may buy a car and give it to you. If you reject me and do not allow me to be your friend, you may miss out on some blessings in your life." My hosts will gently say to me that even though the gift of a car is nice, they still do not want me to bring all my friends into their home to drink alcohol. They would prefer to decline my offer of a car and keep their house quiet and peaceful rather than allow me to do my own thing and create a lot of noise. However much I try to talk to my hosts, they make their decision and I have to respect them.

I could say that they have a very beautiful daughter and when she gets married I will give one thousand dollars towards her wedding if I can invite my friends into their home every evening for alcohol. My hosts may be very thankful for my kind and generous offer but still have to say 'no' because they do not want there to be noise in the home. No matter how much I try to persuade my hosts, they will always say 'no'.

Can you or I persuade God to allow us to reject one of his instructions and still remain in his kingdom? Can we expect God to still give us eternal life in heaven if we will not honour Him in every day and respect every word he says? He is telling us what we ought to do. What are the consequences if we refuse to do what our Father says? Do we really love Him with all our heart if we will not respect Him? Could I enter heaven and say I love everyone, then one day say in heaven that I don't want to love some people? Revelation 21v4 says there will be no crying or pain in heaven, so could God let me enter heaven if I'm going to bring pain there? No. It would not be heaven if it was a place of pain. So we need to know the word of God and honour God's ways all the time.

Ephesians 4v29 tells us not to let any unwholesome talk come out of our mouth. Could I be in heaven and one day say that I never did like Mr X when he was in the same church as me. He always made himself look better than me when he did the Bible reading in the church. I'm going to tell others how he treated me when I am in heaven. Will I be bringing pain into heaven if I talk like this? Am I allowing unwholesome words to come out of my mouth? The Bible says that I should not be doing so. Heaven is a place of everlasting love, and I do not believe God could permit one into heaven if they do not want to show love for all eternity and instead want to put others down in heaven. It would not be a place of love if one was allowed to put others down in heaven.

By encouraging everyone to learn more and more of God's Word, people will become stronger and their faith in God will get deeper and richer. The Bible says in Colossians 3v16 to 'let the Word of Christ dwell in you richly", and when all the people in the church are rich in the Word of God, their love for God will be so deep that they will be delighted to go and share more with others who also need to be equipped for service and built up. God's Word will start to burn in the hearts of people all the time as it did in Jeremiah's heart – Jeremiah 20v9, and a time will come when people will have so much in their heart that they just have to share with others. They will simply long to go and share with others the richness of the scriptures that they know and have become a personal blessing to their own lives. Personal growth for every member of the church family should be the heart of every church leader.

If you are a church leader, what is your motive? Just to teach every Sunday and carry out the regular duties, or to see your people grow to full maturity? Do you want Psalm 119v99-100 to be the goal of the people whenever you teach the Word of God, that the people listening will know more and more of the Word of God?

"I have more understanding than all my teachers: for thy testimonies are my meditation. I understand more than the ancients, because I keep thy precepts." Psalm 119v99-100 NIV

Do you want to release people to teach the Word of God, or just keep them listening to you one year after another? What is your goal for those you teach? Are you really loving God with all your heart and wanting the people to grow, or just carrying out the same religious activities every Sunday but with no burden to see your people grow?

A great danger is that a church can become lukewarm. One can begin on fire for God, but lose the fire and become lukewarm. The church begins in a beautiful way with a lot of passion and a deep burden for the lost. People come together for fellowship several days each week, and the church has regular days of prayer and fasting. There are many opportunities for fellowship. But over the years, the leadership changes, and the next leader may not have the passion that the former leader had. Instead things become simply a routine, so they are fulfilled as a matter of duty rather than from a heart of passion. Meetings are cancelled until the church simply has a Sunday morning service only. There are no prayer meetings or places of fellowship in the week, but just a Sunday morning service. The fire is gone and the church becomes lukewarm.

As we saw in the very first chapter of this book, God does not like a lukewarm church at all. But how does one know that a church is lukewarm if the people have never known what it means to be on fire for God? The result is that the church can simply do things out of tradition, and nullify the Word of God. As Mark 7 says:

'Making the word of God of no effect through your tradition which you have handed down. And many such things you do.' Mark 7v13 NKJV

Every time there is a change of leader, there may be a different attitude to doing God's work. Judges 2v7 shows how the people honoured God during the time of Joshua, but things changed later after the death of Joshua. We read:

"And also all that generation were gathered unto their fathers: and there arose another generation after them, which knew not the Lord, nor yet the works which he had done for Israel. And the children of Israel did evil in the sight of the Lord, and served Baalim." Judges 2v10-11

God wants us to grow. And everyone wants to be greatly rewarded for all eternity. No one wants to suffer loss in heaven. What we need are church leaders who are on fire for God all the time. We never want to see a church become lukewarm. The purpose of the church is to see everyone grow in their relationship with God and one day start to teach others. Never, at any moment, should we allow ourselves to become lukewarm, but always keep the fire burning in our hearts. We should always have a desire to grow and know God more intimately.

But there is another question has to be asked. We may not like the question, but it has to be asked. Are we absolutely sure that we will even enter heaven when we die? Let's look at some more scriptures as we seek to answer this question.

Chapter 7 – Judgement Day

Some people believe you can never lose your salvation. Once you become a Christian, you will know for sure that when you die you go to heaven. Others say that it is possible to lose your salvation and go to hell. In a book called "The Bible Student", the author, Peter Sammons, says that *we must go on believing in order to have eternal life. So it is clearly possible to walk away from eternal life.* What he is saying is that it is possible to lose our eternal life. In another book, "A journey into prayer" by Evelyn Christenson, the author says that Jesus may say on judgment day, *"Depart from Me, you who are cursed" for those who have been cultural Christians, who belonged to fine churches or thought they were God's grandchildren because they had believing parents.*

Whom does one believe and whom does one ignore?

I look at an illustration earlier in this book where a person could join a group of people for lunch on Sunday. Look at this situation.

Someone says, "Can I invite the person to join us for lunch?" Hear some possible reactions from others in the group.

"No, I don't want anyone else to join us. The group is small and I want it to stay that way. If we start to let others join us then I will become very bitter and leave."

"I do not want that person joining us. I have had problems with the person and don't want to talk with them ever again. Personally I hate seeing them and wish they would move away and go to another place."

Could the first person have bitterness in their heart? The Bible says to 'get rid of all bitterness' in Ephesians 4v31. If one does not do so, then are they honouring God, or hardening their heart and refusing to obey God? If they harden their heart, then are they actually loving God with all their heart? Mark 12v30 tells us to love the Lord our God not with *part* of our heart, the *majority* of our heart but with *all* our heart. When part of us chooses to harden our heart, are we actually honouring God?

Look at the other person. The first letter of John talks about the importance of love and has many things to say about hatred in a person. Look at these verses.

"He who does not love does not know God, for God is love." 1 John 4v8 NKJV

If we do not love, we do not know God.

"If someone says, "I love God," and hates his brother, he is a liar; for he who does not love his brother whom he has seen, how can he love God whom he has not seen?" 1 John 4v20 NKJV

We are a liar if we say we love God but do not love someone else.

"Whoever hates his brother is a murderer, and you know that no murderer has eternal life abiding in him."

1 John 3v15 NKJV

Hatred is something God does not like at all, and that is why he says that there is no eternal life in someone when we hate another person.

So we have to go back to our original question in the first chapter of the book. "What is a Christian?" And once again, we can look at the different answers.

One can say a Christian is someone who knows God and has a personal relationship with Him. Another can say a Christian is someone who is committed to a church and shows much loyalty to a church. Another can say that a Christian is someone who believes in Jesus as John 3v16 says. So does 1 John 3v15 apply to anybody? Do we simply believe that one verse, John 3v16, is enough to get us into heaven and that every other verse, including 1 John 3v15, can be ignored? To answer this, let us look at a family.

Can a seven year old child stay awake 24 hours a day for a whole month and never go to sleep? Or does a mother say, in the evening, that the child needs to get changed and go to sleep? If a mother tells a child to sleep, then does that child need to get out of bed in the morning and go to school? Or does that child say to Mum, "I'm obeying you. You told me to go to bed last night and that's what I've done. Let me stay in bed so that I can be obedient to you." Does a child stay in bed for 24 hours a day?

Does someone simply think that 'believing the story of Good Friday' is true is absolute certainty that they will go to heaven? John 3v16 says so very clearly. But, like a mother telling a child to go to bed in the evening, is the child receiving just one instruction from their mum throughout their whole life and never going to do anything else? Will the child never get out of bed to eat or go to school? Will the child remain in the bed for ever and ever?

Do we also just hold onto one word only from God and never listen to anything else that God says to us? Are we just clinging to one statement and nothing else? Or could God be saying to us that 'although you believe in me, I do not like the spirit of hatred you have towards someone else and I want you to get rid of it. If you do not get rid of it, I cannot give you eternal life.'

If a ten year old child is given some money from their parents and told that they can go to the shop and buy some sweets, does the child run away from home and celebrate with his friends that he can do anything he likes? "My parents told me I could go to the shop today. They did not tell me I have to return home. I'm free. I can do whatever I like. I'm so happy."

Will the child stay with his other friends for the rest of his life, or will his friends tell him to return to his parents? How would every parent feel if their child just left home one day and never returned, but decided to stay with other friends? Parents would want to know if their child is safe and how they are doing. Parents simply could not abandon their own children.

Do we, as Christians, think that we also have complete freedom to do whatever we want with our lives? We don't have to love everyone, but are free to hate whoever we want to. We don't have to welcome everyone. We can be bitter towards anyone we like if others don't treat us in a kind way all the time. Why should we get rid of all our bitterness when someone is always borrowing our pen and never returning it? If people are going to be so unkind to us, then they need to know how bitter and annoyed someone can get when they continually ask us if they can borrow a pen yet again from us. We may decide to completely ignore what God our Father is saying and do our own thing instead.

A mother can tell a child to go to sleep in the evening, then tell the child to get up in the morning and get ready for school. And God our Father can tell us that He will give us eternal life in heaven if we believe in Him, then another time tell us that he cannot give us eternal life if we do not get rid of the hatred in our heart towards another person. Life is not based on just one instruction from a parent. Parents tell us many things, when to go to sleep, when to get up and have breakfast, when to wash ourselves, when to do our homework, and many other things. Life is full of many instructions. And the Bible is full of many instructions too.

So the question is, even if we do believe in Jesus, or we do show a lot of loyalty to a church for many years, is that all it requires for us to know for certain that when we die we will go to heaven? Does 1 John 3v15 have any relevance today, or can it just be ignored? What about many other scriptures such as Matthew 25v41? Can this also be ignored on the grounds that we are good in other ways in our lives?

There was a time when I began to think so much about the lake of fire. I imagined many different ways that one could see the reality and pain of hell. I saw a picture of one hundred friends all boiling hot water and putting it into a flask. They would bring their flasks to a room and I sat on a chair with a cloth over my eyes and my arms and legs tied to the chair. I could not move. Suddenly, without any warning, a flask of hot, boiling water was poured over me. I screamed very loudly. 'Stop it. It hurts. Stop it.' But without any warning, six minutes later another friend pours a flask over me. I'd just began to cool down and recover from the pain of the first flask and now I was experiencing the same pain again. I really could not bear it. And so it went on with flasks being poured over me at fifteen minute intervals. The pain was too horrifying to describe.

Another picture was the sun and the earth. The sun rises and is at a certain distance from the earth. But one day the sun was rising and going in a different direction, and was much nearer to the earth. The heat was so great that no one could open their doors and go out. If they did, they would instantly burn from the rays of the sun. It was so hot even just to stay in the home. And no one could leave their home throughout the whole day until the sun went down. To simply go out of the house would lead to death because the sun was so close to the earth. Did I ever want to experience this? Did I want anyone to experience the lake of fire for all eternity? No way. The pain would be too much for anyone to endure. And it would not just be for one or two days. It would be forever and ever.

I would look at judgment day and imagine different possibilities. I imagined someone who has been a faithful, devoted servant in a church for over forty years. One day they die and face judgment. There is one thing in their heart that they could not overcome. They would read the book of Acts and could not let go of the reality of Acts 8v3. They would often say in church that when they get to heaven they will tell Paul that they really did not like the way he used to murder people and be so cruel to them. They somehow feel Paul ought to suffer in heaven for the way he caused others to suffer on earth.

Will they go to heaven? They were very loyal to the church and one of the most generous givers. They did a lot for others in the church, always buying food for the poor families. They cared a lot. Surely God can overlook their attitude towards the Apostle Paul.

No one can say that this person is destined for hell. If anyone deserves to go to heaven it is this person because they showed a huge amount of devotion and commitment to their local church. They were certainly Christian in everything they did, always caring for others. How can anyone possibly think they could end up in hell? What a thing to say.

Yet, on regular occasions, whenever the book of Acts was read in the church, the person always expressed their anger towards Paul. Did they really have hatred in their heart towards Paul? Did they honestly refuse to forgive Paul for how he lived before he became a Christian? If so, would Matthew 6v15 apply to them? Why should God forgive them if they will not forgive someone else?

Would I want to be this person being described in my imagination, with the possibility that I could be the one ending up in the lake of fire? Mark 9v44 says that the fire will never go out. Never. Is hatred just one reason that someone could end up in hell, or are their other reasons too?

Surely, the most beautiful way to answer this is for one to read the entire Bible and see what God has to say about sin, repentance and hell. Do we really think that just to show loyalty to a church, or simply to believe in Jesus (that is, that the Good Friday story is true), is all it requires, or could there be more? Could a personal relationship with God really be the thing that God is looking for in our lives today, that is, someone who loves God all the time, listens to Him and does everything He asks us to do?

Are we absolutely sure we will enter heaven when we die? And if so, will we even be rewarded in heaven? How do we get rewarded? What does God want from us? In the next chapter we will look at some of the ways we can live on earth and their eternal consequences.

Chapter 8 –
God's Measuring Rod

We want to go to heaven. And we will be pleased to have treasures in heaven for all eternity. So let's begin with a question. What is essential in our Christian life and what is optional? Is there any choice in our lives, or is the life we live all about complete submission, and all we do is obey God day after day? Do we have any freedom in our lives?

When I was a teenager, I would watch my parents regularly making a roast dinner for us to enjoy every Sunday after church. I learnt how to make the roast potatoes, and there was a time in my life when I was glad to get up early on a Sunday morning and prepare the Sunday roast for the family. It was a delight to do so. No one forced me to do it, but I chose to do so as a blessing to my parents and sisters.

Sometime later I moved out of my parent's home and lived on my own. No longer was cooking an option for me but it was essential for my health. I had to take responsibility for my own life, so I made sure I bought good, healthy food to cook and eat all the time. I lived alone and had to take care of myself. Cooking was therefore essential so that I had good health.

What is essential and what is optional? Look at fasting. Is it an option or is it essential? There will be times in our lives when important decisions have to be made and we find that the only way to know the Lord's will is to pray and fast and bring the matter before the Lord. Elders were appointed after prayer and fasting as Acts 14v23 says, and Barnabas and Saul were released into the mission field as a result of a time of worshipping and fasting – Acts 13v2-3. Without fasting, it will be very hard at times to know what God is saying and where He is preparing us for. A time comes when fasting becomes an essential part of our life.

At other times we may choose to fast voluntarily for someone or an event. God is blessed when we do something out of a loving, sacrificial heart and simply cannot forget the love we are showing. The depth of love clearly touches the heart of God, and one day we will be rewarded as Psalm 62v12 says. We can choose to do the things that please God and know, for sure, that one day He will reward us. Or we can decline on the basis that we love our food, and also that we do not believe fasting will necessarily help us in the matter. We could end up getting to heaven but suffering loss simply because we declined to do things for God, so he is unable to reward us. We can choose to have a nice, comfortable life on earth, enjoying our food and drink all the time, and spend eternity in heaven with little rewards. Where do we want to invest our life, on earth or in heaven? It's our choice.

How do we measure ourselves? What is our measuring rod that we should use?

Psalm 139v23-24 says "Search me, O God, and know my heart: try me, and know my thoughts: And see if there be any wicked way in me, and lead me in the way everlasting."

We can pray and ask God to shine the torch upon our lives and show us the state of our heart. There are different ways we can look at ourselves. We can examine ourselves by our personal opinion of who we are, or the church's opinion of us, or God's opinion. When it comes to judgment day, it's God's opinion that matters, because He is the one who will decide how we will spend eternity.

Let's leave God aside for the moment and look at the church. The church may speak well of us because of what is visible. A person can be very loyal and devoted to a church, attending every Sunday for many years, helping with the church cleaning and refreshments, and show a lot of commitment to the church. Everyone can therefore believe that this individual is certainly a Christian because of their devotion to the church and acts of service in the church. Does that therefore mean that if the church is pleased with them, then surely God is?

What about our own opinion of ourselves? Our character is good, and we regularly give to the church. We are well financially and have no debts or loans. Our life is certainly blessed. We speak in a polite way all the time, so there is no doubt we are Christian. We are convinced we will go to heaven when we die.

But now look at the Word of God. It is alive and active, sharper than any two edged sword. Hebrews 4 says:

"For the word of God *is* living and powerful, and sharper than any two-edged sword, piercing even to the division of soul and spirit, and of joints and marrow, and is a discerner of the thoughts and intents of the heart." Hebrews 4v12 NKJV

The Bible is God's measuring rod that He uses to judge us. It is a discerner of the thoughts and intents of the heart. Are we committed to Him or not? Do we want to serve Him all the time or not? Are we prepared to repent of every sin or do we prefer to harden our heart? Do we want to take up our cross daily as Luke 9v23 says or do we prefer to decline and please ourselves instead? God uses the Bible to measure our Christian lives. How much are we honouring Him? How much are we doing for Him? His Word becomes the way that he measures our lives.

Do we know the Word of God? Or do we instead prefer others to measure us, and hold onto their opinions instead? Are we using a dangerous measuring rod if we prefer the church's opinion of us, or even our own opinion of ourselves, instead of God's Word? What if we thought we were pleasing God but He was thinking differently? We would never want Matthew 7v23 to apply to us, but the question is, could it apply to us?

This verse says:

And then I will declare to them, 'I never knew you; depart from Me, you who practice lawlessness!' Matthew 7v23 NKJV

Imagine if we could learn the Word of God and measure ourselves by it all the time. Do I listen, or am I the one to talk? See James 1v19. Do I forgive others, or do I hold onto their sins? See Colossians 3v13. Am I humble, or is there a lot of pride in me? See James 4v6. Do I love others, or do I hate my brother? See 1 John 4v20. The more we know the Word of God, the more we can examine ourselves to see if we are living pure, holy lives that bring honour and glory to God, rather than seeking the approval of others around us all the time. 1 Timothy 3v1-6 is another good way to look at ourselves. Are we mature enough to serve as a leader in a church? Do we satisfy these verses?

"This *is* a faithful saying: If a man desires the position of a bishop, he desires a good work. A bishop then must be blameless, the husband of one wife, temperate, sober-minded, of good behaviour, hospitable, able to teach; not given to wine, not violent, not greedy for money, but gentle, not quarrelsome, not covetous; one who rules his own house well, having *his* children in submission with all reverence (for if a man does not know how to rule his own house, how will he take care of the church of God?); not a novice, lest being puffed up with pride he fall into the *same* condemnation as the devil. Moreover he must have a good testimony among those who are outside, lest he fall into reproach and the snare of the devil."

Can you or I say 'yes' to everything listed here? What does this mean for us on judgment day? God sees our hearts and knows if we really love Him all the time and want to please Him or if we are only partially committed and would rather ignore His ways when it enables us to do what we want for ourselves. He knows everything about us. Reading the scriptures over and over again, and learning them, enables us to regularly examine ourselves.

Am I hospitable or do I dislike others and keep a distance from them when I am away from the church premises? Am I generous, or do I like lots of money and like to be rich like others are? Do I have a good testimony or am I known as one who is always noisy at night time and forever having neighbours who complain about me every night? The more we know the Word of God, the more we can examine ourselves. We can begin to learn about ourselves and (1) when our lives are a delight to God and He will reward us, (2) when we decline to serve God and could suffer loss for all eternity, or (3) when we harden our heart towards Gods ways and don't actually love Him with all our heart, even though we think we do. At times we may prefer to please ourselves instead of pleasing God.

Leaders can choose to measure success in the church in different ways. For some, a successful church is one where everyone shows love to others.

"By this all will know that you are My disciples, if you have love for one another." John 13v35 NKJV

When we all love each other, then the church is a very strong family of believers, we may say. We think that our love for each other is the most beautiful way for a church to be. Other leaders can say that a successful church is one that raises up leaders and plants new churches. We are successful because we raise up leaders who go on to do more for God.

Such things can come to light when churches come together for events in the town. A gathering of Street Pastors or volunteers for foodbank helpers can bring together many people from different churches. People start to share about what is going on in their churches. We can learn more about each other and what is going on across the town. Some think in one way and some in another. Who is right and who is wrong? Is church planting essential, or just an option for those who want to do this? Is loving one another enough, even if there is no evangelism and no baptisms in the church? What is the right way to live?

Questions can arise when churches come together and people share about events. One may say that they have had a few baptisms in their church in the last few weeks, and another says that they have not had a baptism for several years now. "It's a number of years since I last did a baptism" says a Pastor. Is this OK, or is the Pastor completely ignoring Matthew 28v19-20? What is acceptable and what is dishonouring to God?

Another church may place a lot of emphasis on the use of our spiritual weapons as 2 Corinthians 10v3-4 says. The church does not want the weapons sitting on the shelf but being put to use at every opportunity. One church may have a week of prayer and fasting every month. Another may have 24 hours of worship, knowing what impact this can have as 2 Chronicles 20v21 shows. One Christian may ask another, "how many times a year does your church have a week of prayer and fasting?" "I've never fasted in my life" the person replies. "Our church never mentions fasting at all."

What is our measuring rod for our relationship with God? Our church leader, or church involvement, or God's Word? What can seem fine in one church may be very hard to accept in another church. How can a church go for an entire year without a time of prayer and fasting? Is the church moving in the power of the Holy Spirit or in its own ways all the time? What is the church doing? Once again, the Word of God will show how it is possible for a church to begin doing something in the power of the Holy Spirit and end up working in its own strength instead, as this verse from the book of Galatians shows.

"Are you so foolish? Having begun in the Spirit, are you now being made perfect by the flesh?" Galatians 3v3 NKJV

What about a new convert? How do we discipline a child or a new Christian? Let's begin with these three verses:

"Train up a child in the way he should go, and when he is old he will not depart from it." Proverbs 22v6 NKJV

"For whom the Lord loves He chastens, and scourges every son whom He receives." Hebrews 12v6 NKJV

"As many as I love, I rebuke and chasten. Therefore be zealous and repent." Revelation 3v19 NKJV

In Revelation 3v19, the New King James Version says 'chasten' and the New International Version says 'discipline'. God wants to chasten us. He wants to discipline us. How does God discipline us? Look at a 12 year old in church. Imagine they are late for the church service. Do we rebuke or forgive?

We have to know the background of the person. Could it be that they are a new convert, and they previously lived with a muslim family but now they have left home and are a Christian? Do we therefore show such joy and delight to see them in the church and welcome them with open arms? Or could it be that the person has been going to church all their entire life, and is now becoming quite rebellious? They want to go outside the church and spend some time with some of their friends before they enter the church, and they start to talk in a way that is very unpleasant to others. Does one discipline them for their bad behaviour?

Now let's look at a person with 300 US$ in the bank. Is this good or is it of great concern to the church? One has to know their background and their activities. Were they once unemployed, but now they have found work and have saved a lot of money in recent weeks? "Well done" we say. "You have worked hard and saved a lot of money. May you have a very blessed future." Or did they inherit a lot of money when a family member died and gave them 10,000 US$? They have been travelling and spending a lot of money on hotels and alcohol and now only have 300 US$ left. They are worried that they will not be able to afford many things in the next couple of months and do not know what to do.

Should the church discipline the person to learn to say 'no' to hotels and alcohol and learn to live within their budget? A lack of discipline could cause such a person to borrow money, get into debt and create a lot of problems for themselves. Surely it's better to discipline the person now before they get into serious financial problems. And regarding the one who was previously unemployed, he should be praised and encouraged to increase his savings so that one day he can move from paying rent to buying his own home. He may be a hard worker and very faithful with his money, and has a lot of opportunities ahead of him to enjoy a very healthy and blessed life.

We have to know the person. We can teach from Matthew 25v1-13 and the dangers of delaying things and not being ready, and leave a lot of fear in a person. What if I am late for church? Could Matthew 25v12 apply to me?

"Afterward the other virgins came also, saying, 'Lord, Lord, open to us!' But he answered and said, 'Assuredly, I say to you, I do not know you.' Matthew 25v11-12 NKJV

We can teach from 2 Corinthians 9v6, telling others that the more generous we are, the more we shall reap. Does the man who had the 10,000 US$ simply give his remaining 300 US$ to the church in the hope that all his problems will disappear and he will soon have 10,000 US$ again? Or should we advise him to write out a budget and give what he believes is a fair sum of money as opposed to giving on the expectation that things will become easy for him in the future? Knowing the person whom we are with is very important so that we know when to discipline and when to encourage them. The verse in 2 Timothy 4v2 tells us to both rebuke and encourage. We have to know which is appropriate for each situation, because everyone is different.

Remember, one day we will face judgment. Will God be thankful because we had godly wisdom all the time as James 3v16-18 says, or very sad because we applied our own wisdom and rejected Gods? We may choose the wisdom that James 3v13-15 refers to and fail to seek the Lord in every situation. When do we rebuke, and when do we encourage? If we want to be rewarded in heaven for all eternity, we can ask God for wisdom all the time as James 1v5 says and be confident He will give it to us. We can choose to follow the Word of God and always ask God for wisdom.

Some may ask, "What is the relevance of all the scriptures?" Let us look at some verses from the book of Psalms.

"Loved one and friend You have put far from me, and my acquaintances into darkness." Psalm 88v18 NKJV

"Reproach has broken my heart, and I am full of heaviness; I looked for someone to take pity, but there was none; and for comforters, but I found none." Psalm 69v20 NKJV

These verses are showing the need for compassion in our hearts towards others. People can feel very lonely and abandoned in their lives.

"You are the God who does wonders; you have declared Your strength among the peoples." Psalm 77v14 NKJV

"It is God who arms me with strength, and makes my way perfect." Psalm 18v32 NKJV

These are verses that encourage us in our daily lives. They remind us of Gods greatness and power.

"Create in me a clean heart, O God, and renew a steadfast spirit within me." Psalm 51v10 NKJV

This is a verse to rebuke us and transform us from our old ways. We do not like our sins and want a clean and pure heart.

Blessed are the undefiled in the way, who walk in the law of the Lord! Blessed are those who keep His testimonies, who seek Him with the whole heart! They also do no iniquity; They walk in His ways. You have commanded us to keep Your precepts diligently. Psalm 119v1-4 NKJV

These verses remind us of God's ways that we have to follow. If we want to live a holy life, we need to follow God's ways.

When I read a chapter in the book of Psalms, I will ask questions. Is there a promise I can receive from this chapter? Is God revealing something to me so that I can show love and compassion to others? I take note of what I read and write down the verses.

As a result, I find myself remembering many scriptures. I can go to an event and observe others around me and look for someone who may be isolated and thankful for some company. God does not like people feeling abandoned and alone and so I can take the opportunity to give time to the one who is all alone. And I delight to do things for God which I know I cannot do on my own. As a result, I'm glad to receive God's promises. They strengthen me in all I do for God. They uplift me. I'm glad to have such good promises that I can hold onto throughout my life.

But is it necessary or beneficial to read the entire Bible? A person may read a chapter in the Bible and ask, very sincerely, 'What's the relevance of these verses?' Look at the first six verses in 1 Chronicles 6.

The sons of Levi were Gershon, Kohath, and Merari. The sons of Kohath *were* Amram, Izhar, Hebron, and Uzziel. The children of Aram were Aaron, Moses, and Miriam. And the sons of Aaron were Nadab, Abihu, Eleazar, and Ithamar. Eleazar begot Phinehas, and Phinehas begot Abishua; Abishua begot Bukki, and Bukki begot Uzzi; Uzzi begot Zerahiah, and Zerahiah begot Meraioth. 1 Chronicles 6v1-6 – NKJV

'What relevance is all his to us today?' someone may ask. God may ask us a question. 'Will you be interested in every single person in heaven? Or do you only want to meet those people whom you knew on earth?'

Have you ever thought about how many people will be in heaven that had no friends on earth? There will be many. Look at a baby that died five days after they were born and entered heaven. Their mum and dad did not get saved and are now in hell. Whom does the baby know in heaven? No one. Will the baby be lonely for all eternity? Or will anyone meet with them and fellowship with them?

'No thanks Lord. I want to meet with my own friends.'

'Lord, I'd rather meet some of the people in the New Testament like the Apostle Paul. I don't really want to spend time talking to babies.'

What if we wanted to enter heaven and reject such babies? What if we made excuses? Everyone who enters heaven is precious to God, whether they lived for 100 years or died when they were in their mother's womb. A mum may have had a miscarriage, or a baby may have been aborted. Does a baby go to heaven, or hell, or nowhere? The Bible says that God knit us together in our mother's womb – Psalm 139v14. That means, the moment the child was conceived, there is life, whether the child is in the mother's womb or the child has been born. Once the child is conceived, there is life. And every living person will enter either heaven or hell.

If every baby under the age of one year enters heaven (because they are too young to understand about salvation), then they will want fellowship in heaven. Do they really want to be ignored and excluded by others in heaven for all eternity? No. That is why God calls us (1) to love everyone and (2) to listen to what the Holy Spirit is saying – Revelation 2v29. The Holy Spirit may be telling us to make friends with some of the people who entered heaven without any friends on earth. 'Go and give them time' says the Holy Spirit. 'Everyone is special to God.'

So when we read 1 Chronicles 6v1-6, we can think of everyone who is precious to God and know that we will meet very many people in heaven who are also precious to God. God will want us to give them time, so we ask the Holy Spirit to dwell in us and show us how to serve God. Remember, we are called to lay down our lives for others as 1 John 3v16 says. We are called to take up our cross daily and follow Jesus as Luke 9v23 says. Taking up our cross means crucifying our own wants and pleasures and choosing God's ways instead. God may say, "Give time to that person." I may say, "I'd rather do this with my day." Whom do we listen to, ourselves or God?

So the entire Bible has very good things for us to receive. Words of encouragement, words of instructions, people's current circumstances and the need for us to give them compassion and love, and words to rebuke us where we are not honouring God in every way in our lives. All scripture is God-breathed, as 2 Timothy 3v16 says. And all means all, even these verses in 1 Chronicles 6v1-6. Every soul is precious to God, both on earth and in heaven. Are we ready, for all eternity, to love everyone we meet?

What's the eternal consequence if we decline to love everyone? 1 John 4v8 is a very serious verse. If we do not love, we do not know God. And if we do not know God, will Jesus say, 'Depart, I never knew you' to us?

'Sorry, I can love Anglicans and Pentecostals but I cannot love those people. I don't like their doctrine. If they get to heaven I will not associate with them because I don't want to get into an argument with them.'

If that's how we think, and we keep a distance from some people but God lets them into heaven, then He sees their beautiful, pure heart, but we may not. Will we be given eternal life in heaven if we love some but exclude others? God will judge us all one day. What could he say? 'You will suffer loss in heaven for all eternity', or 'You do not love because you don't know me, so I cannot let you into heaven.' What could God say? Let us be sure to enter heaven by saying to God that we will love everyone we meet on earth and in heaven and never refuse to love anyone. May 1 John 4v8 never apply to our lives. Let's be sure we will go to heaven by asking God to give us his love for others all the time.

Another question to ask is this. "How precise is God's Word?" Could he really send us to hell if there is one person we dislike or hate? Could 1 John 3v15 apply to us even if we simply dislike just one person and love great multitudes of other people?

When I am driving I see a sign. It says '30'. What does it mean? Does it mean I am only allowed to drink 30 glasses of alcohol when I drive? Is it illegal to drive if I have 31 glasses of alcohol? Or does it mean that I have to be aged 30 or over to drive along a certain road? If I am 29 or younger, would I be banned from driving in this place? What does the '30' mean? It means that drivers are not allowed to exceed 30 miles per hour (mph). 30mph is the maximum speed limit along this road. And there is a speed camera ahead.

Ten drivers all drive at a different speed along the road? The question is, how many of them will get a speeding fine for breaking the speed limit? Look at the results of all ten drivers.

29.999mph

30.000 mph

30.001 mph

30.002 mph

30.010 mph

30.100 mph

30.900 mph

30.999 mph

31.000 mph

31.001 mph

How many will get a speeding fine for not driving at 30mph or less?

Will the person driving at 30.001 mph be given a speeding fine? He drove faster than 30.000 mph. What about the person driving at 30.900 mph? He drove faster than 30.000 mph but less than 31mph, so he could argue that he should not get a fine. How precise are the people when they say that fines will be issued for those who drive faster than 30mph? The sign does not say 30.3 or 30.5. It says 30 which means 30.000. If the sign said 30.0 then it would imply that no one can drive faster than 30.0 mph, but it does not say this. So surely someone driving at 31.000 should be given a speeding fine for exceeding the speed limit. Just how precise are people in society?

What about a train departing from London at 10.47am? Will I be able to board the train if I reach the platform at 10.48am, or at 10.47.05 am? Or will the doors be shut and the train already departing from the platform at precisely 10:47:00? How precise does one have to be in order to ensure they don't miss the train?

Does a driver want a speeding fine? The way to ensure that they do not get a fine is to drive at 28 or 29 mph so that they are absolutely confident that they will not exceed 30mph. And does a person want to spend eternity in hell? The way to ensure that they do not go to hell is to honour the Lord and his ways and never allow hatred to dwell in their heart for a single moment. If it does start to enter a person's heart, one should rebuke such a thought immediately and ask God for unconditional love for the person. Remember, Jesus told us to love our enemies, so we have to ask God to give us love all the time and not allow any hatred to take root in our lives. To do so could be putting our lives at risk.

God did not make us like mobile phones. With a mobile phone, you can find someone's name, press a button and the phone starts to call a person. You choose who to contact and the phone follows your instructions. God does not put a mobile in our hearts and press buttons to instruct us to do things. Can you imagine if we only obeyed instructions all the time. "Give a word of encouragement to Abel today at 9am. Give a meal to Bob at midday. Give a phone call to Christopher at 3pm. Pray for David at 6pm." We are not like mobile phones, simply obeying instructions all the time. We have freedom to choose what to do every day. If God did make us like mobiles, we could be absolutely sure we never exceed the speed limit ever. We always slow down and drive within the legal speed limit. But God gives us choices all the time, and we can choose what to do with our lives. And it's our choices that determine where and how we spend our eternal lives.

Are we pleased that God has given us freedom, or would we prefer to be like robots, always being obedient to every single instruction? God has given every one of us the freedom to choose how to live, and we should choose Him above every other thing on earth. What could be the risk, the eternal consequence if we decide, at any time in our lives, to reject God's ways?

What are the consequences if we drive for over ten years along a road at 30mph, and one day we drive at 35mph? Will we escape a speeding fine on the basis that we have been good for the last ten years? Or will we still get a fine? What are the consequences if we always pay for our food every time we enter a supermarket, then one day we decide to steal a lot of food and do not pay? Will we escape the Police? Or will we face punishment for stealing from the shop? Can many years of good deeds give us the authority to break the rules and escape punishment?

Can lots of good deeds and kindness allow us to escape the lake of fire on judgment day? How precise is the world today when it comes to speeding fines and punishment, and how precise is God when he tells us to honour Him in every way in our lives? Let's return to the question at the beginning of this chapter. What is essential and what is optional? How does God measure us? What does God think of us?

"Do we have to have a prayer meeting in the church? Do we need a weekly Bible Study? Or is it OK to go along to the church just once a week on a Sunday?" The question we have to ask ourselves is, 'Am I looking at everything from an intellectual point of view, or do I look at things from the heart? Do I serve God out of duty, or with a heart of delight?' Look at this verse.

"So let each one *give* as he purposes in his heart, not grudgingly or of necessity; for God loves a cheerful giver." 2 Corinthians 9v7

This verse clearly shows a distinction between doing something out of necessity and doing something cheerfully. One can give their money or their time to something simply as a matter of duty, thinking that they have to do things in order to show they are a Christian. Others can do things because they enjoy being a blessing. They serve out of a heart of delight. Love should always be our motive rather than the law. Paul says in the letter to Philemon that he would rather something is done out of love than out of compulsion.

"But without your consent I wanted to do nothing, that your good deed might not be by compulsion, as it were, but voluntary." Philemon v14.

What could cause us to do things out of compulsion? We may want to join the church choir, so we feel compelled to help with the church cleaning because we want to be seen as a committed member of the church and therefore be allowed to sing in the choir. If we do not help with the cleaning, some may question if we are really committed to the church. Cleaning can prove we are committed. We don't clean because we delight to make the place so beautiful for the church family, but because we are seeking favour from the church choir.

Why do we read the Bible? Out of duty or out of delight? Look at all these scriptures about the Word of God.

I have not departed from the commandment of His lips; I have treasured the words of His mouth more than my necessary *food.* Job 23v12 NKJV

"I have written to you, young men, because you are strong, and the word of God abides in you, and you have overcome the wicked one." 1 John 2v14 NKJV

"Let the word of Christ dwell in you richly." Colossians 3v16 NKJV

"The wise men are ashamed, they are dismayed and taken. Behold, they have rejected the word of the Lord; So what wisdom do they have?" Jeremiah 8v9 NKJV

"I know that you are Abraham's descendants, but you seek to kill Me, because My word has no place in you." John 8v37 NKJV

Moreover He said to me: "Son of man, receive into your heart all My words that I speak to you, and hear with your ears." Ezekiel 3v10 NKJV

Do we really love God's Word more than our daily food? Could we be killing Jesus because his Word has no place in our lives? Are we using God's wisdom or our own wisdom? Does our heart receive all the words God speaks to us? Not a fair proportion of the words or the majority, but all the words God speaks to us, as Ezekiel 3v10 says? '*All* my words' says Ezekiel 3v10. '*All* my words.'

The Bible is the best measuring rod we can use to look at ourselves. Everyone, yes all of us, will one day face judgment. Which is better, to hope that we will enter heaven or to be certain? Do we want to 'think' we are following God, or know for sure, that we really do have a wonderful relationship with God? Another question to ask is this. What is law, and what is a personal choice? What do we have to do, and what can we *choose* to do?

Chapter 9 - Owning a Car: The Law and Freedom

Everyone has questions in their minds. People can think a long time about some things on their heart. Should I do this? Is it OK if I say 'no' to something? Am I expected to attend somewhere now that I am a Christian? What should I be doing with my life?

Illustrations and examples can be a good way to answer some of our questions. In this chapter we will look at what it means to be a car owner, and compare this with what it means to be a Christian.

Owning a car in the UK means I have to follow certain laws. Let's look at these facts.

1. I have to pay for car insurance and car tax (UK law).
2. I am encouraged to regularly clean my car (my respect for others).
3. I can go long distances and visit many places (my vision for the year ahead).

In the UK I cannot choose to buy car insurance. I have to. It is the law. When my insurance is due for renewal, I'm breaking the law here in the UK if I decide I do not want to pay for another years insurance and still continue to drive the vehicle.

Similarly, as a Christian, I will go to hell if I do not repent and be obedient to everything God tells me to do. "Unless you repent, you will perish" says Jesus – Luke 13v5. To accept Jesus as my personal Saviour means to repent of every single sin. And to be a car owner means I will always be insured. The Police can arrest me here in England if I drive an uninsured car. And God can send me to hell if I refuse to repent of every sin.

I can choose to clean my car. I can clean it every day, once a week or not at all. Whatever I choose, I am not breaking the law. The Police can do nothing to me if I decide to go for a whole month without cleaning my car. Even if my neighbours complain how filthy my car is, they can do nothing. Reporting me to the Police will not help in any way.

However, there is something very different for a Christian. We need love. "Without love, we are nothing," says the Bible - 1 Corinthians 13v3. When I show love, I choose to clean my car so that others can have a lift in a vehicle that is both clean and well maintained.

But let's look at this. One can be very conscious of caring for others to the extent that not only do they clean the car but they put lots of bottles of water in the car for all their passengers. They really show a lot of love and care to those whom they give a lift to. This is a delight. It is a personal choice and it is a blessing to God and to others. However, imagine there is one thing they need to deal with. They are very forgetful when they have to pay for their car insurance. They keep forgetting to do so and several times they have been fined for driving an uninsured car. Very soon they will lose their driving licence and not be allowed to drive again. It's great to have a loving heart but it cannot become an excuse for failing to abide in the law.

And it's great for Christians to have a loving heart too, showing much generosity and kindness towards others, but we must never forget God's laws. They are there to be obeyed and we must always do so. The words of Jesus must abide in us at all times (John 15v7) so that we can honour God all the time. Without the Word of God abiding in our hearts, we can so easily forget God's ways.

And also, as a car owner, we have the privilege of driving to many places. We can travel, see new places and meet other people as opposed to being limited to those we can walk to or visit by public transport. And as Christians, we have the opportunity to do more and more as we grow closer to God. God never expects us to remain babies, always reliant upon milk year after year. He expects us to grow, to receive solid food (Hebrews 5v14), and to go and take the gospel to others (Matthew 28v19-20).

A wife may want to travel across the UK to see her son at university. A husband may reject the idea, preferring to save money instead. A heavenly Father may ask his children to do something for Him. A Christian may decline the invitation. Is there any intimacy between ourselves and God, or are we just living a life of limited vision and lacking a lot of love and respect for anyone else? Are we prepared to go, or always holding back because of the cost? Where is our love for others and our faith in God?

So as a car owner, there are important things to be aware of. Firstly, I have to obey the law. I must insure my car. Secondly, I am encouraged to keep my car clean at all times. It shows respect to others. Thirdly, it is good to go to places and enjoy good relationships with others. We can show much love to others and store up more and more treasures in heaven. The alternative, restraining ourselves from travelling (even just leaving the comforts of our homes), will limit our relationships and people can turn cold towards us. We could turn cold towards God. We could even lose our first love. We will look at this in Chapter 11.

And as a Christian, all three points are important for us all.

We have to repent to get into heaven. We cannot escape hell if we refuse to repent of every single sin. We should also show love at all times. What good is self-righteousness without love? (See Luke 18v11-12). Even the Apostle Paul could say he was faultless, but he was not satisfied with himself. He wanted to know God more.

"As for zeal, persecuting the church; as for righteousness based on the law, faultless. But whatever were gains to me I now consider loss for the sake of Christ." Philippians 3v6-7 NIV

And we should be active for the Lord. God wants to reward us for all eternity. But always remember that without faith it is impossible to please God – Hebrews 11v6. We are called to serve God and obey him. We should not hold back because of fear or caution.

But there is a big question we all have to ask ourselves. Where does the cross fit into all this? Is it compulsory, or a choice? Are we expected to take up our cross *daily*, or can we choose to do so as we wish? Do we see taking up the cross like the car insurance, something we must have all the time, or like the car cleaning, something we can do if we wish to? How do we see the cross?

Taking up our cross

How many crosses do we look at in the Christian life? We say that there is only one cross and that is the one that Jesus died on. But Jesus tells us to take up our cross – Matthew 16v24. The question is, are we doing so? Are we ready to deny ourselves and take up our cross?

Galatians 2v20 says "It's no longer I that lives." Have we died to ourselves? Have we?

The Lord gave me a picture. I got a piece of paper and wrote down the two words "Sin" and "Evil". What one letter is common to both words? The letter "I".

Put these two words together on a cross with "I" as the letter at the centre:

```
            E
            V
    S   I   N
            L
```

Now God says "repent". If we do not repent, are we born again? Will we go to heaven if we do not repent? God says "repent" so turn the cross over and write the word "evil" in the opposite direction, and leave out the letter "I". "I" has to die. We have to die to ourselves. It's no longer "I that lives" – Galatians 2v20.

```
            L
    S       I       N
            V
            E
```

What do you get when you repent, when "I" has died? There is nothing left of self – nothing. What is nothing? It is '0'. Put nothing in the cross. It is none of self and all of Christ. See the result:

```
            L
    S       O       N
            V
            E
```

Eternity Beckons – Are You Ready?

The Son of God, full of love, died so that we could receive forgiveness of sins and eternal life in heaven. Is the cross valid if "I" is there? Can we expect to go to heaven if "I" does not want to die?

"I do not want to give to the Lord. I'd rather keep my money for myself. Still, I'm a good Christian."

"I want to stop witnessing and have a year at home enjoying TV. I'd rather enjoy my own company. Still, I'm a good Christian."

Has "I" been crucified? Does "I" continue to live, or can I declare that "it's no longer I that lives?" Gal 2v20.

Our love for God should be so deep that we, the Body of Christ, die to ourselves all the time and give our lives to God. We should be interested in Jesus all the time and ask him, "what do you want me to do for you? How can I bless you? How can I serve you?" When we really do ask God how we can serve Him with all our heart, he will tell us from the Word.

Look at some of God's answers in these verses:

"And He said to them, "Go into all the world and preach the gospel to every creature." Mark 16v15 NKJV

Go therefore and make disciples of all the nations, baptizing them in the name of the Father and of the Son and of the Holy Spirit, teaching them to observe all things that I have commanded you; and lo, I am with you always, *even* to the end of the age." Amen. Matthew 28v19-20 NKJV

In the same way that we have to pay our car insurance here in the UK, so God expects us to take up our cross daily – Luke 9v23. We have to know, as Christians, what God expects of us every day. We may learn this, but how easy is it do to so?

Cleaning our car is an option, but paying our car insurance is the law. What about praying, giving and fasting? Are they options? Or are they all law? Does God expect us to pray, to give and to fast, or are they all a choice? Does God expect us to evangelise, or is this a choice? Does God expect us to welcome people into our homes, or is this a choice?

Jesus says in Matthew chapter 6, when you pray, when you give and when you fast. He does not say if you pray, if you give or if you fast. He assumes, because we follow Him, we will do all these things. Because we say we love God with all our heart, God can expect us to do all these things. And because we say we will buy a car, one can expect us to pay our UK car tax and insurance.

Similarly, if we want to travel somewhere in our car, we will be expected to buy fuel for the journey. And if we want to be one of Jesus' disciples, we are expected to take up our cross. If we don't pay the price for the fuel, we cannot drive a long distance in the car. And if we don't pay the price of following Jesus and take up our cross, and we really able to call ourselves a disciple? Jesus will ask us to do many things that we may not like. But, if we want to follow Jesus, we have to obey Him all the time.

Many times God can be asking for changes. He wants us to do something new. The question is, is our heart softened and willing to change in every situation, or is our heart hardened and resistant to change? What is our attitude towards God? Do we look at everything under the law, or out of a heart of love? Do we say to ourselves, "I don't have to clean my car. And I don't have to pray. I'm not going to let anyone force me to do such things." Or do we say, "I love Jesus. He's so wonderful. I just want to do more and more for Jesus. I really want to bless him." How do we look at things? From a matter of the law, or out of a heart of love?

When you look at things from a heart of love, you recognise how God may be looking for changes in a situation. Look at some of these verses and see some of the changes that God may be longing for in our hearts.

Permissible, but beneficial?

"I have the right to do anything," you say—but not everything is beneficial. "I have the right to do anything"—but not everything is constructive. 1 Corinthians 10v23 NIV

A person goes to a supermarket and buys one item at a time. They buy bread and walk home with the bread, then leave again to buy milk. They get the milk, take it home then return to the supermarket again to buy bananas. Carrying one item at a time is easier than carrying lots of things at once. But, if the person gets a bag and puts the bread, milk and bananas in the bag, then everything can be carried all together. It saves a lot of time. Yes, buying every item separately is permissible, but is it beneficial or constructive?

Are we using our time in a way that is constructive, or simply doing things that look good when actually we are using a lot of our time to do many different things? We have a choice. We can carry on doing the things the way we do them, or we can listen to God and change our ways.

Coldness

I have been asked to look after the church refreshments. I made a decision to make the cups of tea and coffee on the Saturday evening and leave them in the church for the Sunday service. The tea and coffee is cold the next day, but at least everyone can have a drink. How do people feel? People may not be happy. They feel I am acting in an unloving way.

I say, "I am the one in charge of the refreshments, so you have to accept what I decide to do. A cold cup of tea or coffee is better than having nothing to drink at all, so just be thankful."

The Bible says the love of many will grow cold – Matthew 242v12. How does God feel with a church full of people with cold hearts?

No power

I have been asked to look after the church refreshments. I made a decision to cut off the electricity so that we do not have a big electricity bill to pay ever again. I'm saving money, so everyone will have a glass of water from now on.

How do people feel? People may not be happy. They feel I am acting in a stingy way and refusing to boil the kettle just to save a little bit of money.

God has given us power, and that power is given to be used – Luke 10v19. But do we see things happening in our churches as Luke 10v19 says? God does not like a church that denies his power, and tells us to have nothing to do with them – 2 Timothy 3v5 - NIV. The KJV says that we are to turn away from such people. Do we obey God, or ignore Him and act without God's power?

No faith

I have been asked to look after the church refreshments. I made a decision to cancel the church refreshments completely. I do not want to find the church running out of money and unable to pay the electricity bills and we end up sitting in a very dark building in the evenings. I cannot see how we will survive financially in the weeks ahead.

How do people feel? People may not be happy. They feel I am over reacting and going to the extreme of looking at everything we spend money on.

God tells us to live by faith and not by sight. Without faith it is impossible to please God- Hebrews 11v6. And yet I chose to cancel the refreshments completely. How many things have been cancelled in our churches because of a lack of faith? Do we have enough money for mid-week Bible studies and prayer meetings, or are we afraid of a big electricity bill, heating bills and the extra cost of additional refreshments? Do we live by faith anymore?

Humility

I have been asked to look after the church refreshments. I made a decision for my friend to look after the refreshments for the next three weeks as I will be away on holiday. People have to wait a long time for their hot drinks because my friend is always making phone calls and not getting on with the refreshments. Some have offered to do the refreshments next time I go away, but I say 'no.' I decide whom to delegate to as I'm the one in charge.

How much pride is in me? Do I need to humble myself and accept counsel and guidance from others? How much pride is in our churches today where people will not accept counsel and advice from someone else? The Bible tells us to humble ourselves - 2 Chronicles 7v14.

Are we living in a generation where we think that a lot of these things don't really matter? So long as our personal finances are in good order and we get by week after week and we simply attend church, surely there is enough evidence to say we are Christian? Does the content of the Word of God really matter that much? Or are we living in a generation where we have a very shallow understanding of the

Word of God, and are not bothered too much about things? The ultimate question is, "Do we love God with all our heart so that we want to honour the Word of God completely, or do we think a partial commitment to the Word of God is sufficient to escape hell and go to heaven? What does it mean today to love the Lord our God with all our heart?"

How much do we love God? With the majority of our heart, or with all our heart? Do we see all these illustrations as small matters that can be ignored, or things that are important and very much on God's heart, and hence that is the reason they are in the Bible?

Are we prepared to listen to God? Do we want to listen to our Father, or simply expect God to listen to our prayers all the time? Do we see the need to read the Bible every day, or do we see this as an option like cleaning our car? If we don't read the Bible daily, could we be ignoring God's voice and therefore not actually loving him all the time?

A heart that is hardened in places may see no need for growth and not know the richness of reading the Word of God on a daily basis. They simply do not know the beauty of drawing closer to God and knowing Him more and more on a personal basis. God is seen more as someone whom people have to submit to, rather than a Father whom they can relate to and be friends with.

Many times God can be asking for changes. He wants us to do something new. The question is, is our heart softened and willing to change in every situation, or is our heart hardened and resistant to change?

One day we will face judgment. What will we say to God? "I did not have time to read your Word because I was always doing things on earth. I was never lazy, but always active the whole time." What if

God said that you could have used your time in a better way so that you made more hours in the day to read My word, but you just remained set in your own ways all your life? How would you or I feel to hear such words spoken to us on judgment day? Let us ask ourselves if, though everything we do is permissible, it is actually beneficial and constructive? Maybe we need to pray and ask God to soften our heart and show us what changes He would like in our lives.

Another change that God may want is for us to come out of the world. But we fear to do so because we do not want to be hated by others. In the gospel of John we read this:

"If you were of the world, the world would love its own. Yet because you are not of the world, but I chose you out of the world, therefore the world hates you." John 15v19

We do not want to be hated, so we prefer to do things that get the approval of others. We would rather get the approval of others than please God and be hated by those around us. The world is used to sin and lies, and when we speak the truth we risk being hated by the world. "I will not lie and accept money. I will speak the truth" we may say. If we follow God and speak the truth, we run the risk that others may dislike us because we expose their sins. If we all sin together and lie about something, then we think that perhaps we can all be blessed.

We may think that this is a choice like cleaning our car rather than a command, but the Bible says that we are 'chosen out of the world'. Is it time for God to soften our heart so that we become the salt and light in society instead of conforming to the ways of the world?

Another challenge in churches can be attitudes, which are often as a result of past teachings. People can have different views of the church. Look at this example. There are twenty people in a church, and fourteen people like to join us for fellowship on a Monday evening but six are always absent. Two people can view this with completely different attitudes.

"It's so wonderful to see fourteen people coming together. I'm really pleased with the fellowship."

"Why do some come on Sunday then always stay away from the other meetings? Where's the commitment of people?"

Why do they have different attitudes? For one person, they learn not to get hurt or disheartened. They have no expectations or burdens, but simply appreciate all they have and all that God has given them, and are just thankful all the time. Fourteen people is better than no fellowship at all. It's a blessing.

For the other, they always remember being taught John 13v34. Love is a command, not a choice. We are called to love one another.

A new commandment I give to you, that you love one another; as I have loved you, that you also love one another. John 13v34 - NKJV

We are called to think of others above ourselves (Romans 12v10 – NIV). If you really are a Christian, you will always think of others first of all. The person therefore feels disappointed that some seem to be ignoring such commandments.

Such a person could have been 'forced' to do something as a young child, believing that this was how every Christian was expected to live. "You have to do that. You must do this." We are 'commanded' to love one another. Others do things spontaneously. Who is right, and who is wrong.

But without your consent I wanted to do nothing, that your good deed might not be by compulsion, as it were, but voluntary. Philemon v14 – NKJV

The weak you have not strengthened, nor have you healed those who were sick, nor bound up the broken, nor brought back what was driven away, nor sought what was lost; but with force and cruelty you have ruled them. Ezekiel 34v4 - NKJV

When do we do things freely, from the heart, and when are we expected to do certain things? It's an important question. Should we just all avoid any disappointment and take the view of the first person, that we simply live a thankful life every day, never expecting anything? If we have this attitude, we will never be disappointed. Jesus noticed that only one 'leper' said 'thank you' to him. If we expect nothing from others, then we can 'rejoice' when one person does say 'thank you'. We feel blessed in life. If we expect all ten to say 'thank you' and only one does, we can feel disappointed with the others. What is the best attitude to have in life?

The most healthiest and best attitude to have is to say that 'I will always bless Jesus and do whatever He asks me to do so that daily I can honour Him and give glory to Him. Instead of saying that I don't have to do something, I will always say that I delight to do this for God.' So if I can say 'thank you' to someone and bless them, then I will. But I will not hold it against others if they refuse to show any thanks to me when I serve them in some way. I just delight to serve God.

Psalm 37v4 says 'Delight yourself in the Lord.' Psalm 112v1 talks about someone finding *great delight* in God's commands. Yes, great delight. We can reach a point where God is so beautiful that we just love to give Him everything, like the widow who gave away her last coin. What a delight, when we reach a point in our lives where God is so beautiful that we just want to honour him all the time and do indeed take great delight in serving God and in his commands.

We have a choice. Every day we can look at things from the point of the law. It is true that I have to pay car insurance but I do not have to clean my car, so I can decline to do so. Or we can look at things from the heart all the time. I love to bless others and bless God so I will clean the car and make it look nice. It's always a joy to do things for others and for God. Let us choose to look at things from a blessed way all the time. Let us not cling to the law and use it as an excuse to decline or delay to do something. Let love be the motive for everything we do. Let's choose love above the law.

We can choose the law and suffer loss in heaven for all eternity. We can choose to do everything in love and be richly rewarded for all eternity. Let's think about our eternal life and always be motivated out of a heart of love.

Hebrews 6v10 says that God will not forget the love you have shown. God greatest delight is not about you keeping the law all the time but about the love you show. It is the love you show that will bless God both now and for all eternity.

Eternity Beckons – Are You Ready?

These two poetic illustrations are inspired directly from the pages of Mary K Baxter's books, titled "A Divine Revelation of Heaven" and "A Divine Revelation of Hell"....

Heaven

Peaceful, holy, radiant, pure:
Through jewelled gates on golden floor,
Where blissful scents of angel throngs,
Attend the air with children's songs.
Each sick, miscarried, blighted soul,
Runs blemish-free: complete and whole.
And with their laughter, sunshine rays,
Ascend on high as holy praise.
Unmeasured splendour, fit for Kings,
Now opens up through angel wings,
As vibrant flowers and vivid green,
Offset this brilliant, blinding scene.
Sparkling gems adorn the street,
While mansions rise where diamonds meet,
And beauty shines from every view,
Reflecting back its light on you.
Then, as you're called before the throne,
To meet the God you're spirit's known,
No words depict nor book can share,
The awesome love that meets you there......

Juliet Dawn

Richard Smart

Hell

Putrid, pungent, rancid, vile:
The belly of hell presents its bile.
Tormented cries and anguished moans,
Decaying flesh and blackened bones.
Insidious worms that stake their claim,
To what was once your living frame;
Fraying joints and sinew dregs,
Were once your earthly arms and legs.
Holes for eyes and claws for fists,
Your soul a swirling, dirty mist.
Mocking laughter, piercing spears;
Demonic sport, eternal years.
Constant burning, ceaseless pain,
That sends your knowing mind insane.
A stenchful home of brimstone pits;
Consuming flames in starts and fits.
Here memories of yesterlife,
Intersperse regret and strife,
And when all fragile hope has gone,
This endless hell, just stretches on..........

Juliet Dawn

Part 2:
Revelations from God

Over the years I would set aside a lot of time to read in order to understand many things and draw closer to God. There was such a deep desire within me to understand more about God and his ways. And certain books had a big impact on my life. One book in particular was called 'Driven by Eternity' by John Bevere. On page 97 it says:

"In the late 1980's, God gave me a spiritual vision. I saw a multitude so large that you couldn't see the end of it. It was a sea of humanity. I knew there were no atheists in this group, no self-acknowledged sinners, no followers of other religions; rather, all confessed being Christians through the lordship of Jesus. This multitude had come to the Judgement and were fully expecting to hear Jesus say, "Enter into the joy of your Lord; the kingdom of God." But instead they heard the words, "Depart from Me, you who practice lawlessness." (Matthew 7:23)."

The book said how everyone expected to go to heaven. But instead they heard the words 'depart from me'. So I asked a question. How much does the New Testament talk about repentance and hell? I had a real burden to study the Bible, and as a result I would more and get many revelations.

Lack of submission to God was just one way that we could be rebelling against God by refusing to listen to Him and obey Him. The Bible says that we ought to be teachers and yet perhaps we were refusing to teach others what we ourselves had learnt. We may not be submitting to God as he asks us to. I could see why the picture that was given to John Bevere could apply to so many of us today.

Reading through the New Testament, I began to understand more and more of the ways of satan. I could see the truth in this verse in 2 Peter, how the scriptures were being distorted at times.

He writes the same way in all his letters, speaking in them of these matters. His letters contain some things that are hard to understand, *which ignorant and unstable people distort, as they do the other Scriptures, to their own destruction.* 2 Peter 3v16 NIV

The devil used scriptures to tempt Jesus to sin, and we have to be careful that we do not allow scriptures to distort us for our own destruction.

Another book that had a big impact was 'Husbands and Fathers' by Derek Prince. On page 139 there is a paragraph headed 'Christianity or Churchianity?'

The paragraph says, *"Churchianity produces members; Christianity produces disciples. Churchianity demands conformity; Christianity demands commitment. The great majority of professing Christians today are not even aware of their departure from the original pattern and standard of the Gospel. They have simply formed their concept of Christianity from what they see in the contemporary Church."*

Derek Prince says in this book that the great majority of professing Christians are not aware of their departure from the original pattern and standard of the Gospel. After reading this, I wanted to understand the Word of God more and more. What if I was one of those who had departed from the original pattern standard of the Gospel?

I devoted many hours to studying the scriptures, and would write down many things that God was showing me. In the following chapters are some of the revelations I received from God.

Chapter 10 –
A Wrong Interpretation of Humility and Unity

We shall look at Numbers 13v30-33. Let us study this passage.

Then Caleb silenced the people before Moses and said, "We should go up and take possession of the land, for we can certainly do it." But the men who had gone up with him said, "We can't attack those people; they are stronger than we are." And they spread among the Israelites a bad report about the land they had explored. They said, "The land we explored devours those living in it. All the people we saw there are of great size. We saw the Nephilim there (the descendants of Anak come from the Nephilim). We seemed like grasshoppers in our own eyes, and we looked the same to them." NIV

Caleb believed that they *could* possess the land. Caleb had faith in God. But was this right? The rest of the people all believed that they could not do so. They did not think they were able to possess the land and they said so. And this pleases God (so people think). Look at these two facts.

1. God resists the proud, but gives grace to the humble. 1 Peter 5v5 NIV.

2. There are six things that God hates. One of them is a lying tongue.

"There are six things the LORD hates, seven that are detestable to him: haughty eyes, a lying tongue, hands that shed innocent blood." Proverbs 6v16-17. NIV

The good thing is that the Israelites were honest. They did not lie and say 'I know we can possess the land." Instead they honestly admitted how they felt. They said that they seemed like grasshoppers. Honesty is good, and as the book of Proverbs says, God hates a lying tongue. The Israelites did not lie – they spoke the truth. They said how they really felt.

And secondly there was no pride in them. They did not boast about what they could do. God hates pride and the good thing is that there was no pride in them at all. So the Israelites must have been good in the eyes of the Lord. They were honest, not liars, and there was no pride in them.

Caleb, however, could appear to be a man full of pride. He claimed that they could indeed possess the land. "We can certainly do it", he said. There he was, saying what he believed could be done. Does

God like people who are big headed and always boasting about what they can do? Yet here was Caleb, boasting about how much he believed that they could go and possess the land. Which is better, to be a person full of pride who always boasts about what they can do or to be a person of humility who recognises how weak they are and confesses what they are unable to do? "God *resists* the proud", says the Bible, and we have to make sure that we do not let pride get into us.

Another good thing is that the Israelites were united together as one. They all agreed together that they did not believe they could go and attack the people (verse 31). Unity is good, and where there is unity, God will command his blessing. Look at Psalm 133:

"How good and pleasant it is when brothers live together in unity! It is like precious oil poured on the head, running down on the beard, running down on Aaron's beard, down upon the collar of his robes. It is as if the dew of Hermon were falling on Mount Zion. For there the LORD bestows his blessing, even life forevermore." Psalm 133v1-3 – NIV.

When there is unity, God commands his blessing. This Psalm says so. And certainly the Israelites were in unity. The New Testament tells us about the need for unity in Ephesians.

"Endeavouring to keep the unity of the Spirit in the bond of peace." Ephesians 4v3

And the Israelites could certainly look at each other and say that they were in unity. They all agreed that they did not want to go and possess the land because they simply did not believe they could do so. The only person who was not in agreement with them was Caleb.

So, to conclude, the Israelites were not lying; they were telling the truth. The Israelites were not full of pride. They did not for a single moment boast about what they could do, and they were in unity. They really stood together as one body.

As one looks through the Bible, one starts to look at other characters. Was there pride in David? He felt he could defeat Goliath, yet no one else had dared to make such a claim. Why should David stand out from the crowd and be different from the rest, and not learn to agree with others? God loves unity.

When one looks at the importance of humility and the dangers of pride, the importance of unity and its benefits (Psalm 133), and the importance of telling the truth (remembering just how much God hates a lying tongue), surely one can conclude that God must be pleased with the Israelites. Regarding Caleb, it is down to God to judge him if he doesn't want to be in unity with the others and cannot be truthful like the others. However, for the rest of the Israelites God must be very pleased with their response. They are truthful and honest.

At that time no one knew how God would respond. When you read Numbers 13v30-33 you do not know how God will respond in the following chapter. What you do know, however, is that God loves honesty and that the Israelites did not lie to him. That you do know.

And today no one knows what God will say to them on judgement day. We all hope and trust that we will be welcomed into heaven. "We are indeed Christians", we say. We sing songs in church such as "Thine be the glory, risen conquering son", and so declare that Jesus is indeed risen. Why would we declare something if we didn't believe it? The very fact that we sing it shows that we believe in Jesus, that he died and rose again, so we know we are going to heaven. We don't worship other gods. We worship Jesus so we know we are Christians. Heaven is where we are going.

What is wrong with such a way of thinking? To judge the church and say that it could be wrong is not a nice thing to do because we, as Christians, are called to be kind to others. Look at Colossians 3v12:

"Therefore, as the elect of God, holy and beloved, put on tender mercies, *kindness*, humility, meekness and longsuffering." NKJV

We are called to clothe ourselves with kindness. Telling the church that it could be wrong is not considered to be a kind thing to do, and people therefore learn to remain quiet. We like to be polite and show respect to those around us so we choose to be careful in what we say. We learn to act in a kind way, as this verse in Colossians says.

But where does rebuking come into the body of Christ? Look at Proverbs 28v23 and Revelation 3v19.

"He who rebukes a man will in the end gain more favour than he who has a flattering tongue." Proverbs 28v23 – NIV.

"Those whom I love I rebuke and discipline. So be earnest, and repent." Revelation 3v19 – NIV.

God wants people to come out of their lukewarmness and to go deeper with him. That's why he says, "Those whom I love, *I rebuke*." He wants us to have a beautiful relationship with him. But do we need to rebuke others today? Is rebuking relevant at such a time as this?

If God is pleased with us, then surely he is happy with all that is going on in our churches and we can rest in peace. And surely if the Israelites had no pride in them and they were honest and said how they really felt, then God must be pleased with them too. Is there any need to rebuke the Israelites when they seem to be living in a very honest way? There doesn't seem to be any pride in them. It looks as though they are fine as they are.

Like the Israelites, who said that they simply did not think they could possess the land, we too can say how we feel. Caleb chose to be different, but for the rest of the Israelites they came to a mutual agreement that it was going to be hard to attack the people. Was Caleb right to think like he was, or were the Israelites right in their way of thinking? Who was God pleased with? We have to make a decision. Can we, for a moment, imagine God would be pleased with the Israelites and not with Caleb because Caleb did not learn to fit in with the rest of the people? One man simply refused to stand with the others. He refused to.

Now imagine God was pleased with Caleb but not with the rest of the Israelites. Caleb was willing to go and possess the land whereas the others simply did not think they could. Could God be pleased with Caleb and not with the rest of the Israelites? As one examines the scriptures, (not having any pride, not lying but being honest at all times and learning to be in unity), the most likely conclusion is that God is pleased with the Israelites. They really expressed how they felt and were in unity.

And today, so long as the church is in unity, there should be every reason why God is pleased with us too. God should be pleased with his church and we should be able to enjoy every day confident that we will go to heaven when we die. But there is a very big danger here when you look at this way of thinking. The danger is that we could be twisting the scriptures to satisfy our own ways. Look at 2 Peter 3v15-16:

"Bear in mind that our Lord's patience means salvation, just as our dear brother Paul also wrote you with the wisdom that God gave him. He writes the same way in all his letters, speaking in them of these matters. His letters contain some things that are hard to understand, which ignorant and unstable people distort, as they do the other Scriptures, to their own destruction."

Are we distorting the scriptures today? Are we heading to our own destruction, to hell? Are we? No one would want to think that God was not pleased with the Israelites. Their unity and their honesty must have been very wonderful to God and given him such joy, and the only sad point is the unwillingness in Caleb to accept the viewpoint of all the others. Caleb simply did not want to be united with the rest of the Israelites, and God loves unity.

Some of us may never have read beyond chapter 13. We have absolutely no idea what God's response will be. Only when one reads into the next chapter does one find out how God judged the people. What was God's response? Numbers 14v23-24 tells us:

"Not one of them will ever see the land I promised on oath to their forefathers. No one who has treated me with contempt will ever see it. But because my servant Caleb has a different spirit and follows me wholeheartedly, I will bring him into the land he went to, and his descendants will inherit it." NIV

Can this possibly be true? "Not one of the Israelites will ever see the promised land. Not one." They were honest, they did not lie and they were in unity. How could God therefore say what he said?

And when we all appear before the judgement seat of Christ, could God say the same about his people today? Are we ready, or will the church be shocked by God's response? Does God's response totally contradict the way we have been thinking? Is the church in a very big deception today?

Facts:

1. God *promised* the Israelites that they would be taken into a land flowing with milk and honey – Exodus 3v8.

2. God is not a man that he should lie, or the son of man that he should change his mind – Numbers 23v19.

So if he has promised that the Israelites will enter the promised land, then how could Numbers 14v23 say what it says? "Not one of them will ever see the land I promised on oath to their forefathers. No one!"

What I learnt was that a promise given by God requires our faith in Him and our actions. How can God let the Israelites enter the promised land if they will not believe Him and trust Him completely as Caleb did?

Can God keep his promise to us and allow us to enter the land if we refuse to trust him wholeheartedly and never act in faith? Is Christianity to be compared with a baby, forever expecting Mum and Dad to do everything and never being willing to leave Mum and Dad and go to school away from their parents? Are we forever expecting God to do everything and never willing to believe Him when he tells us we can go and possess the land?

'Mummy, ever since you gave birth to me you have fed me, washed me and kept me warm. I know you but I do not know the school teachers, so I cannot go to school because they might not love me like you do. Can I stay at home and be with you forever?'

Imagine if we never went to school. Would we have skills and friends? And what if we never act and walk in faith and start to trust God? Will we be told we cannot enter heaven because we refused to trust God? Could we end up in hell because we were cowards in God's eyes? What does the Bible say about cowards?

But the cowardly, the unbelieving, the vile, the murderers, the sexually immoral, those who practice magic arts, the idolaters and all liars—they will be consigned to the fiery lake of burning sulfur. This is the second death." Revelation 21v8

How easy is it to be like Caleb, focussed completely on God and always wanting to obey God and finding yourself surrounded by others to share a different opinion? Are we really willing to be different to those around us and trust God in every situation, regardless of what others think?

Could unbelief be one of the areas in our lives that we have clung to and not given to God? Could this be something God is waiting for, and until we give it to Him, he knows that we have not fully surrendered ourselves to Him and therefore cannot use us? Can we expect eternal life in heaven if we choose not to repent of one or more sins? This is a question we all need to ask ourselves.

Humility is not about admitting where we are weak. It's about trusting in the Lord with all our heart and leaning not on our own understanding. To say we 'humble' ourselves by admitting what we cannot do is implying that we do not have faith in God. This is not humility, but unbelief. And to say that God loves unity is not completely true if we agree with something that is against God's will. Unity is only a blessing when we are pleasing God all the time.

Chapter 11 - Our First Love

In the book of Revelation we read this:

"Nevertheless I have somewhat against thee, because thou hast left thy first love." Revelation 2v4

What is our first love? If I were to ask the question, 'what is our first love?' in a church, I wonder what answers people would give?

Let us look at this illustration of what it means to be loved by someone.

A hundred years ago my friend Bobby age 24, decided to swim for two hundred days in the sea. Every day he woke up at 4am and went swimming for an hour each morning. He raised £120,000 and decided to give all the money to me so that I could buy Bibles for my friends in Africa. He chose *me* to be the beneficiary of the money he raised. I could not believe how, out of all the people he knew, he chose me. I was so touched, so overwhelmed by Bobby's love for me, that I can never forget what he did for me. I will never stop loving him and thanking him for what he did for me. I cannot put it into words how thankful I am for Bobby.

If his children need any help I'm always glad to assist at every opportunity. I cannot say 'no' to Bobby or his family when they have done so much for me. Even when he is older and celebrating 60 years of marriage, I will still remember him and his family. I can never forget Bobby because of what he did for me.

So in this illustration, what is my first love? It is this:

"I can never forget what he did for me. I cannot say 'no' to Bobby or his family when they have done so much for me."

And God says this. "Now compare what Bobby did for you with what my Son Jesus did for you. Who paid the greater price?"

'Jesus did. He saved me from hell. He suffered on the cross and died for me.'

Just look at what Jesus did. What did Jesus do? God could have looked at the earth and held back his only Son. "I shall not send him to earth. I know people will hurt my Son, say very unloving things to him and show hatred toward him. I cannot let my son go through such torment. I'm keeping him in heaven with me."

"I know that means the people on earth will enter hell when they die, but I cannot allow my son to suffer the way he will on earth. I have to keep him here with me. I have to."

Is that what God did? No, he *sent* his only Son. He *sent* him. And Jesus faced a lot of suffering. Look at what Jesus endured.

"And rose up, and thrust him out of the city, and led him unto the brow of the hill whereon their city was built, that they might cast him down headlong. But he passing through the midst of them went his way. " Luke 4v29-30

"The people answered and said, Thou hast a devil: who goeth about to kill thee?" John 7v20

We see how people tried to take Jesus' life, and how others said that he has a devil.

Let's keep looking through the gospel of John:

The Jews answered him, "Then answered the Jews, and said unto him, Say we not well that thou art a Samaritan, and hast a devil?" John 8v48

"And many of them said, He hath a devil, and is mad; why hear ye him?" John 10v20

"Then from that day forth they took counsel together for to put him to death." John 11v53

People said that Jesus had a devil. Others tried to put him to death.

Look at what Jesus is facing in his life. Should Jesus still go and die on the cross? He's had such a lot of suffering already. Should he really have to face even more suffering, or should he give up and ask his Father to take him back to heaven? How much more suffering will Jesus have to face? Just how much, and will he be able to bear it?

"But this cometh to pass, that the word might be fulfilled that is written in their law, They hated me without a cause." John 15v25

People were saying how much they hated Jesus. Yet Jesus was full of love and wanted people to repent of their sins, follow Him and go to heaven when they die. Jesus wanted the best for everybody. However, people were saying how much they hated him. How unpleasant, to have to face so much hatred from people in your life.

Which is better, to give up whilst Jesus is strong, or to continue and find that the journey gets so tough that He cannot face any more sufferings? What is best for Jesus?

"Then they said, "Hail, King of the Jews!" And they struck Him with their hands." John 19v3 NKJV

People were now hitting Jesus in the face. What had Jesus done to deserve this? People were saying wicked things about Jesus; others were trying to take his life, and now people were hitting him in the face. Should Jesus really continue and go all the way to the cross, or should he end everything and go back to heaven?

Let's look at the options:

If he gives up, he will not have to face any more earthly suffering and he can enjoy peace in heaven. We will all die and go to hell because there will be no one who can die on the cross for us and make a way for our sins to be forgiven. We will have to enter the unbearable fire of hell, which will never end. We will all live in the unbearable fire of hell forever and ever.

If he continues, he will defeat the powers of darkness and make a way for us all to be able to go to heaven when we die. But to continue will mean further suffering and having to be nailed to a cross. To continue is going to mean much further pain for Jesus.

Jesus had to face this decision.

"And he went a little farther, and fell on his face, and prayed, saying, O my Father, if it be possible, let this cup pass from me: nevertheless not as I will, but as thou wilt." Matthew 26v39

Let's ask ourselves a question. If Jesus decides to go all the way to the cross and die for us, how will we feel when we look at Jesus? I believe we are all deeply thankful for the price Jesus paid for us on the cross. And we have to ask ourselves, 'Can we say these very words to God?'

"I can never forget what he did for me. I cannot say 'no' to Jesus or his Father when he has done so much for me."

That is your first love. But are you forgetting what you said when you realized what a great price Jesus paid for you on the cross? Are you forgetting the price Jesus paid for you?

Let's now return to the illustration of Bobby at the beginning of this chapter. He did something wonderful for me. I simply cannot forget what he did for me. Could I possibly reject Bobby when I have two pens, and he asks if I have a spare pen to give him? Could my heart allow me to say 'no' to Bobby? Of course not. I'll always love him after all that he did for me. I'll always love him.

In Matthew 18v23-35 we read the parable of the unforgiving servant. We read how one person was forgiven for a very big thing, and yet he could not forgive someone else for something much smaller. In the end, he was put in jail because he refused to forgive the other person for the smaller debt. Such a parable clearly shows how we can so easily forget about all that others have done for us. We can so easily hold someone else to account for their small activity, completely forgetting that someone has forgiven us for something far bigger. Could I forget about Bobby's kindness to me and decide, one day, not to give him my spare pen? Look at this:

"I gave Bobby a meal last week and a cup of coffee yesterday. Today he is asking me if I have a spare pen. Why should I keep on doing things for him? Why doesn't he learn to carry his own pen with him? What's wrong with him?" How could I, or anyone else, suddenly turn against someone who did such a beautiful thing for me all those years ago? And how can we, God's people, forget all that Jesus did for us? The parable of the unforgiving servant so clearly shows what is possible for us all.

There was a time when God gave me a picture that has never left me. One day the Holy Spirit said to me;

"Go to the seafront and look at the sea. Imagine the sea turns into a lake of fire. Stand and look at the lake of fire for one whole hour. Simply look at the flames. Do you now understand how much my Son did for you when he died on the cross for you? He saved you from the eternal fire of hell because he *died* for you. He *died* for you to save you from the fire of hell."

When we never lose our first love, when we constantly think of the price Jesus paid for us on the cross, we will be delighted to listen to God. Ezekiel 3v10 says 'Take to heart *all the Words I speak to you*." We will be delighted to take to heart everything God says to us. We will take to heart *everything* He says because we love God so much.

The more we look at the lake of fire, the more we should be so thankful for Jesus dying for us that we simply delight to serve Him and honour Him every moment of our lives. Pleasing God should be the greatest blessing for us all the time. And the more we look at the life of Jesus and all the suffering he went through, even before he went to the cross, the more our hearts should be so touched by his love for us that we simply enjoy blessing him all the time. No longer do we ask ourselves if we 'have to' do something, but instead our hearts are so thankful and forever full of gratitude that we simply delight to do things for God. There is a difference between feeling obliged to do something and doing things out of a heart full of thankfulness.

It's not about having a good memory or how intelligent we are. It's about our heart and our love for Jesus. It's about loving Him so much that we always want to serve Him. We can never say 'no' to God. We simply cannot lose our first love. If we do not know what our first love is, we may try, in our own strength, to retain the messages and learn more and more of the Bible. But when our first love is forever in our heart, we do not need to try and hold onto the word. Our hearts are captivated by God's love and cannot fail to retain every word that God tells us. May we be so consumed with the love of God that we take to heart *every Word God speaks to us* – Ezekiel 3v10.

Chapter 12 –
A Wrong Definition of Love

Galatians 1v6 talks about another gospel. It says "I am astonished that you are so quickly deserting him who called you in the grace of Christ and are turning to a different gospel." What could this other gospel be?

Could it be a gospel that says God loves me even if I do not read the Bible? Do we live in a world that says my spouse loves me even when I only wash once a month? I know my spouse loves me, so it does not matter how often I wear the same clothes. I know I will always be loved by my spouse.

Can the church say to me that it does not matter if I evangelise or not? I know I will always be loved by my Heavenly Father. Are we presenting a gospel that says it's OK to be unclean? We know we are always loved, so it's fine to remain unclean. There is a price to pay if we want to become clean. Soap and shower gel are not free. Electricity is not free if we want to use the washing machine. And there is a price to pay if we want to evangelise. Things are not free in our world. We have to pay a price.

Let's look ahead to a new year. Sunday will be the first day of a new month and a new year. Let's agree that we will all cut down on the time and money we spend on laundry. We will all wash ourselves on the first day of every month, then wear the same clothes for the rest of the month and next wash on 1st February. In 2017 we shall limit ourselves to twelve washes during the year, always on the first day of every month. That way, we save time and money.

How will people feel if they sit next to me in a meeting on Sunday 22nd January 2017? They may well get up and move elsewhere because there is a stench in the room. I have not washed for 21 days and wherever I go, people know there is a stench. I end up sitting alone in a lot of meetings. More and more people leave the meeting before it is finished.

Could there be a stench in the church today? I feel justified in not washing on the grounds that I'm saving time and money, but others do not feel pleased sitting near me. Does the church feel justified in saving time and money by cutting down on evangelism so that we do not get into financial difficulties? I can honestly say that if I spend less money in 2017 on soap and shower gel, I will be able to save for other things. The church can also justify saving money by doing less evangelism.

How does God feel if we do not wash ourselves spiritually? We wash ourselves in order to be spiritually clean.

"Christ also loved the church, and gave himself for it; that he might sanctify and cleanse it with the washing of water by the word. " Ephesians 5v25-26

And when we read the Word, we take to heart the last words in the gospel of Matthew. We "go therefore and make disciples of all nations, baptizing them in the name of the Father and of the Son and of the Holy Spirit, teaching them to observe all that I have commanded you."

Matthew 23v27 tells us that we can look clean on the outside, but in the heart there can be many things that are unclean. We may say, "But does it matter?" Is it important to be clean? Or do we prefer to be told that we are saved by grace, through faith, as Ephesians 2v8 says, so we don't feel it matters how we are? "Jesus paid154 the price for us all when he died on the cross" we may say, "so what difference does it make if we are not clean on the inside?" Is it absolutely important to be clean on the inside, or can we live just the way we are, knowing that Jesus died for us? Is it important to be spiritually clean? Is it important to read our Bibles and let the Word of God abide in us? Do we understand the need to be clean today, or do we not consider it important in the eyes of God?

If my wife tells me to go to the supermarket and buy some soap and shower gel, I may do so. But what good is it if I leave it in the shopping bag and never use it? What good is it if we read the Bible but leave the scriptures in the book and never allow them to enter our hearts and be put into action? Could we be creating a stench in our own lives?

Let's not just look at the cost of soap and shower gel in a supermarket and decide to cut down on expenses next year. Let's not buy the goods and leave them in the shopping bag. Let's buy the soap, put it in the shower room and use it *daily* to make ourselves nice and clean and be a blessing for others whom we fellowship with. And let's open the Bible, read the Word and let it enter our hearts and be acted upon so that we are a really beautiful church for God to use, a church whom God delights in. Let us stop reasoning as to how we can save money and let us be ready to wash ourselves all the time and do the work that God has called us to do. Let us "go therefore and make disciples of all nations, baptizing them in the name of the Father and of the Son and of the Holy Spirit, teaching them to observe all that I have commanded you."

My definition of love to my wife may be very different to her definition of love to me. I may say that "I'll reduce the number of days I'll wash myself so that I cut down on the cost of soap. I love you, and I'm trying to cut down on spending so that we save money." My wife will say, "If you love me you will wash yourself daily so that you keep nice and clean." Could our definition of how we love God, that is, not spending money on events in order to save money, be a very different way to the way that God expects us to love Him? Could God be expecting us to read the Word of God more and putting it into practice? We don't just hear the Word, but we do as it says. See James 1v22.

Could it be that we are indeed listening to another gospel, a message that says that we do not have to do anything because Christ did it all when he died for us on the cross? We see no need to read our Bibles at home or go and evangelise? Instead we simply submit to our church rules so that we keep the church functioning from one year to the next? Could this be why Derek Prince says that there is a clear difference between Churchianity and Christianity?

Is the love that God is asking from us perhaps far deeper than the love we give Him?

Chapter 13 –
Quick to Accuse Others

A 'Joshua 22' experience...

There was a time when I read through the book of Joshua. I would read a few chapters a day and make notes. When I read chapter 22 there was a lot going on and I wanted to understand the chapter so I read it again and again. As I did I learnt something wonderful in this chapter. It is very easy to be misunderstood, and it's so wonderful when people can explain why they do what they do in order that everyone is able to understand each other and be in unity.

When I read the chapter up to verse 18, it looks as though something terrible has taken place. In verse 13 it says 'so the Israelites sent Phinehas...'. In verse 16 we read that he said to them, "How could you break faith with the God of Israel like this? How could you turn away from the Lord and build yourselves an altar in rebellion against him now?" As you and I read this, it sounds as though the people have committed a sin and need to repent. The words 'How could you break faith with the God of Israel' are not encouraging words at all. What an unpleasant thing to be told.

What do you do when you personally hear such words? I like to give an explanation and let others know why I am doing something. I don't want to be misunderstood. If we read the rest of the chapter we see that the outcome was good, but before we do so, I'd like to share some things.

It's so easy to draw our own conclusions without praying about the situation and asking God for wisdom. Anyone could listen to the words spoken by Phinehas and share them with another person. "Did you hear what Phinehas said to those people? He said how they turned away from the Lord. I think that's a disgrace. Why do they do such things?" That's gossip, which God doesn't like (Romans 1v29), but how often do we do it? We think there is something wrong with a person and we tell others for whatever reason we wish to. We justify ourselves because 'we warn to warn others what this person is like, especially after the way Phinehas spoke to them' and we think we're right.

Why is it that someone wants to do something they are told 'no' and yet others are allowed to do the same thing and gets a lot of praise for it? If I talk about a particular thing I may possibly get a very unpleasant reaction from someone, so I keep quiet but find myself walking around with a sad face. My body language can say a lot about the way I feel. There can be times when you or I may well feel that something is not right, but what can we do about it?

People can be very clever and know how to falsely accuse someone else. Imagine a person goes to work or college and someone says to them, "Can you lend me your pen?" The person responds with kindness and lend their pen to the other person. They wait patiently for the pen to be returned and keep waiting. Eventually they tell someone else that this person is not returning their pen. They say, "This colleague asked if they could borrow my pen and I'm still waiting for it to be returned to me. Can you help?"

The other person says, "I did not ask you if I could borrow your pen? Don't lie about me."

That is true. The person said, "Can you lend me your pen?" They did not say, "Can I borrow your pen?" Whom does your friend believe, you or your colleague? Who is telling the truth and who is being deceitful? Are you lying about someone else, or did they really ask to borrow your pen?

Let's continue to read the rest of the chapter. What happened in Joshua 22 from verse 21 onwards? The people were able to respond. They were given an opportunity to talk and they were listened to! They wanted to do what they believed was the right thing and explained themselves. Look at the response from Phinehas in verse 31. "Today we know that the Lord is with us, because you have not acted unfaithfully towards the Lord in this matter." Phinehas said something positive. Wow! He said the people had 'not acted unfaithfully.' So when one person gossiped to another about what Phinehas first said, they had not waited until the people had been given a chance to speak up for themselves.

No wonder God doesn't like gossip. We may say things without praying about the matter before hand, and don't take time to find out about the heart of the person. I believe many people want to do many good things in their lives but are afraid of being falsely accused of doing something wrong. People would rather drop away from church and live their own quiet life than remain in a church and encounter more criticism and false accusations. We see, in Chapter 15, how people rebuked a woman harshly (Mark 14v5) and yet Jesus was pleased with her, saying she had done a beautiful thing (verse 6).

Would you like false accusations being made about you? "This person accessed me of keeping his pen when I never asked to borrow a pen from him. He lies about people. I know he does." The person asked someone to lend them their pen. They did not mention the word 'borrow', so they can easily accuse someone of saying something this is not correct. "I never asked if I could borrow their pen, and I don't like these false accusations. I will not allow anyone to spoil my name." Would you like to be expelled from college or fired from a job all because someone is lying in order to keep their reputation or their position?

How many people have been into a church and felt rebuked for something when their motives were to do good? Have you had a Mark 14v5 experience? Do you need a 'Joshua 22' experience, where you have a chance to share yourself with others, so that the matter can be resolved and others will respect you for what you did.

Look at verse 33 – "They were glad to hear the report and praised God." What a happy and peaceful outcome. Phinehas and his team listened carefully to what the others had to say, and everyone became happy and praised God. God's heart is for us all to have a *Joshua 22* experience, where we can listen to one another and come to a peaceful conclusion. A peaceful outcome is what everyone longs for all the time.

Is there a way to get out of this wrong mindset? How do we change things so that people can grow in the church and have a deeper relationship with God? One important part of church life is leadership. Ephesians 2v20 has to be honoured so that a church will grow into maturity and do all that God has called it to do. When we all reach maturity, we can resolve everything in a loving way that is for the blessings of everyone. Let's move on and look at church leadership.

Chapter 14 – Apostles and Prophets

We read this in the book of Ephesians.

"Having been built on the foundation of the apostles and prophets, Jesus Christ Himself being the chief cornerstone." Ephesians 2v20

As we look at the situation in our churches, many questions arise. Are we seeing growth, or are some churches closing? Why is the church where it is? Why do people keep leaving our churches? How does God feel? What does he want us to do? Many questions may pass through our minds.

Look at the following picture:

Richard Smart

The small box represents the present position of the church. People are contented and accept where they are. But the larger box represents the bigger size of the church that God longs for. He has much work for the church to do, and is looking for people to serve him in new ways, in new places.

The people inside the small box simply cannot understand why those outside are calling them to increase their works. They simply do not see the logic or purpose of doing more for the Lord. "Why is it so important?" they ask themselves. "We're saved by grace, not by works, as the Bible says, so let's just learn to enjoy things the way they are."

But apostles and prophets see things far differently. They see the whole picture, as revealed to them by God through his Word, and they know God wants the church to do more for him. The church is founded on Apostles and Prophets as Ephesians 2v20 says, but today the apostolic anointing is rarely spoken of in the church. And prophets are seldom given their proper place in the church. Look at 1 Corinthians 12v28:

"And God hath set some in the church, first apostles, secondarily prophets, thirdly teachers."

If a church has a wrong foundation, namely Pastors, then it can only see inside the small box. It has no reason at all to look beyond the box. People think that a Christian is someone who believes in Jesus and does good. Think about it. Why would the church be full of evil people when Christians live good lives? So as long as we are good we know we are Christian. We therefore are very good and sing when we are told to and sit when the sermon is being shared, so people can see how good we are in the church. We know, without a doubt, that we are Christian. Heaven is where we are going when we die. We are therefore at peace and relaxed with things. Why, therefore, look at growth?

Look at these scriptures:

"Enlarge the place of thy tent, and let them stretch forth the curtains of thine habitations: spare not, lengthen thy cords, and strengthen thy stakes. For thou shalt break forth on the right hand and on the left; and thy seed shall inherit the Gentiles, and make the desolate cities to be inhabited." Isaiah 54v2-3

"Again he measured a thousand, and brought me through the waters; the waters were to the knees. Again he measured a thousand, and brought me through; the waters were to the loins. Afterward he measured a thousand; and it was a river that I could not pass over: for the waters were risen, waters to swim in, a river that could not be passed over." Ezekiel 47v4-5

What is the relevance of spreading out to the right and to the left? Why go deeper with God? Who really wants to end up out of their depth?

Without the Apostolic and Prophetic anointing in the church, such scriptures will not make a lot of sense to the people. The church is quite contented with the way things are. People are friendly to one another and generally behave in a very good way. They can be quite contented with things knowing with total certainty that they are going to heaven. People will think that enlarging your tent or going deeper with God is only something that you do should you feel it right to do so, because this doesn't apply to everyone.

But God's Word is for us all to read, and we should all ask God to speak to us through His word all the time. And Apostles and Prophets see very clearly the need to do more for the Lord. There are many souls that need to be saved, many people that need healing, much work to be done in the world today and we can never sit back and simply be contented with the way things are.

Can we really say, any of us, that we love God, if we have no desire to obey him and do his will? "Enlarge the place of your tent", says the Lord, but are we listening to him? Can we say we love someone if we refuse to listen to them? Is that love? Without Apostles and Prophets, we simply become used to the way things are and have no burden or urgency to see things changed. Could it be that we are deceived into thinking that we are going to heaven just because of the work that Christ has done on the cross for us?

Yes, God has given us the gift of eternal life through Christ Jesus our Lord (see Romans 6v23), but are we really loving God and serving him? Are we just takers, simply expecting to receive the gift of eternal life *from* God, or are we givers, surrendering our lives *to* God and really desiring to love him wholeheartedly and obey him at every moment because we delight to serve him?

Many people in the church today may be so used to being under a Pastor that they cannot begin to understand the way an Apostle serves God. They simply do not understand the apostolic anointing. Going deeper with God simply is not a concern to them, so why are others so passionate about the church drawing closer to God? It isn't necessary, so they think, and cannot see the need to spend more time in prayer or in the Word.

Apostles see the need to do much more for the Lord and that is why we cannot rest. They see the need for people to be healed and delivered so that they are pure in heart and totally well and in good health, and we see the need for the poor to be helped so that we can love our neighbours and give them better standards of living and enable them to receive the blessings that we enjoy in our lives. They don't just look at the problems but go to the root of the problems and so get people delivered. Once the roots are dealt with, then the problems are gone and people can enjoy the blessings. But today very few people go to the roots of the problems. They simply do not have the apostolic anointing.

By entering the established church, we can simply continue to wear ourselves out and get more and more tired and exhausted. As the Psalm says:

Unless the Lord builds the house, they labour in vain who build it." Psalm 127v1 NKJV

We love the people but yet we cannot seem to help them to know the truth. The Pastoral head simply does not know or recognise the apostolic or prophetic anointing and cannot therefore welcome such people into positions of leadership. The Pastor keeps his ways firm in the church and so the church ends up operating on the principles of man and not God's ways. 1 Corinthians 12v28 is rejected and simply not applied. Few people realise why it needs to be applied.

The result is that the established church needs to have a complete change of thinking. The mindset of the church needs to be renewed, as Romans 12v2. There is a clear difference between an Apostle and a Pastor. God loves them both, but the Apostle is the one with the higher anointing whom God has called to be part of the foundation of the church. Let's remind ourselves that the church is:

"Built upon the foundation of the apostles and prophets, Jesus Christ himself being the chief corner stone." Ephesians 2v20

What is the difference between a Pastor and an Apostle? Look at Saul and David:

"And David said to Saul, Let no man's heart fail because of him; thy servant will go and fight with this Philistine. And Saul said to David, Thou art not able to go against this Philistine to fight with him: for thou art but a youth, and he a man of war from his youth." 1 Samuel 17v32-33

Saul loved David and did not want him injured or killed. Saul cared for David. He has a Pastor's heart. David looked to God and to God alone and believed that with God's help he could defeat the giant. David did not look at the giant; he looked at God with whom he could *defeat* the giant! David had the apostolic anointing. Clearly there is a difference between concern for safety (a Pastors heart), and confidence of victory with God's help (the Apostolic anointing).

Now look at Peter and Jesus.

"From that time forth began Jesus to shew unto his disciples, how that he must go unto Jerusalem, and suffer many things of the elders and chief priests and scribes, and be killed, and be raised again the third day. Then Peter took him, and began to rebuke him, saying, be it far from thee, Lord: this shall not be unto thee." Matthew 16v21-22

Peter cared for Jesus and did not believe that Jesus deserved to die on the cross. Jesus had turned water into wine and given sight to the blind, and everything Jesus did was good, so Peter did not want Jesus to be killed. But Jesus had the highest anointing and did what His Father called him to do. At that moment Peter had a Pastor's heart. And churches may not give the right kind of love if they do not operate on the foundation of Apostles and Prophets. The love of a Pastor (protection and safety) is very different to the love of an Apostle, encouraging people to use their gifts and to fulfil the vision God has given them. One protects (the Pastor); the other releases (the Apostle).

Who else had the apostolic anointing in the Old Testament? Look at Caleb:

"And Caleb stilled the people before Moses, and said, Let us go up at once, and possess it; for we are well able to overcome it." Numbers 13v30

But the men that went up with him said, "we be not able to go up against the people; for they are stronger than we." v31

Caleb did not look at the giants; he looked at God with whom he could *defeat* the giants! Caleb had the apostolic anointing.

What was God's response?

"They certainly shall not see the land of which I swore to their fathers, nor shall any of those who rejected Me see it. But My servant Caleb, because he has a different spirit in him and has followed

Me fully, I will bring into the land where he went, and his descendants shall inherit it." Numbers 14v23-24 NKJV

Very often Pastors can stop God's work from being done. The Sauls and the Peters who have a Pastoral heart may easily stop the work from going ahead. We need Apostles to lead our churches, not Pastors.

Apostles stand on the promises of God. Look at some of God's promises.

"I will lead the blind by ways they have not known, along unfamiliar paths I will guide them; I will turn the darkness into light before them and make the rough places smooth. These are the things I will do; I will not forsake them." Isaiah 42v16 NIV

"When you pass through the waters, I will be with you; and when you pass through the rivers, they will not sweep over you. When you walk through the fire, you will not be burned; the flames will not set you ablaze." Isaiah 43v2 NIV

"I will go before you and will level the mountains; I will break down gates of bronze and cut through bars of iron." Isaiah 45v2 NIV

"The Lord will keep you from all harm. He will watch over your life." Psalm 121v7 NIV

Apostles welcome such words. Pastors may reject them though fears and uncertainties about situations.

God wants to give us the nations.

"Ask of Me, and I will give *You* the nations *for* Your inheritance, and the ends of the earth *for* Your possession." Psalm 2v8

"He has declared to His people the power of His works, in giving them the heritage of the nations." Psalm 111v6 NKJV

Prophets are also very important in the life of the church. Prophets bring correction when it is necessary. Look at these scriptures:

"Let a righteous man strike me—it is a kindness; let him rebuke me—it is oil on my head. My head will not refuse it." Psalm 141v5 NIV

"He who rebukes a man will in the end gain more favor than he who has a flattering tongue." Proverbs 28v23 NIV

"Whoever loves discipline loves knowledge, but he who hates correction is stupid." Proverbs 12v1 NIV

It can be very easy for a church to move away from the will of God and do its own thing. Prophets can help everyone to stay focussed on the work that God has and continue to please God all the time.

God is looking for the right foundation in every church. Without this in place, the church may be of very little use to God. Let's look at a plane. When it is about to come to the end of the journey, it needs a good runway to land on. A runway has to be straight and smooth. A plane cannot land on a beach where there are a lot of stones and groynes. The plane will not move along the beach because of the stones and get damaged when it hits a groyne. The plane needs a runway with a good, strong, smooth foundation so that it can have a safe landing. And God needs churches with the foundation of Apostles and Prophets before he can use his church for His purposes. What good is it saying that there is a big stretch of beach where planes can land if the beach is not smooth and has groynes in the way? And what good is it inviting people to gather together for regular activities on a Sunday in a church if the church has not got the right foundation? Will the plane land safely? Will the church-goers grow in their Christian faith and know God's ways?

How much of the church today lives by sight and not by faith, the very opposite of 2 Corinthians 5v7? We may calculate our activities based on our annual budget, and do what we believe we can afford to do rather than what God is calling us to do. We lack faith and instead live by sight. What is not of faith is 'sin' says the Bible – Romans 14v23.

How much can we actually do for God if our hearts repent completely and we are full of God's love? How much can we ask God for when we pray?

Faith to move mountains

Look at Mark 11v23. The bible says that faith can move mountains. But how many? Can we pray for five mountains to be moved by God? Or ten? Or even 100? What limit does God put on us?

"Have faith in God," Jesus answered. "I tell you the truth, if anyone says to this mountain, 'Go, throw yourself into the sea,' and does not doubt in his heart but believes that what he says will happen, it will be done for him." Mark 11v22-23 NIV

When one studies the scriptures, one realises just how much God can do. 5 loaves and 2 fish can feed not 50, not 100 but 5,000 people. Solomon had not 2,000 helpers or 15,000 helpers but 153,600 helpers, (2 Chronicles 2v17-18). God is big. There are many times when he does things in a big way. As Ephesians 3v20 says:

"Now unto him that is able to do exceeding abundantly above all that we ask or think, according to the power that worketh in us."

So there is *no limit* to how many mountains one can move as they live wholeheartedly for *Him*, do everything for His glory and pray in His name. God can move very many mountains.

So the first question is, "Do we have faith in God?" If we do have faith, then what is our vision? What are we believing God for?

And the second question is not 'how many mountains will God move?' but 'why do you want them moved?' The motive of our heart is very important to God, as this verse says.

"All a person's ways seem pure to them, but motives are weighed by the Lord." Proverbs 16v2 - NIV

One needs to examine themselves and ask what they long to do for God and why they long to do it. When the only reason one is doing something is for the glory of God, then God will give us all that we ask for so that He gets all the glory, as John 14v13 says. We get no glory at all and do not want any, because we only live for God and for God alone. All that we do is simply because we love him, and we love him *because He first loved us!* So it doesn't matter whether God releases nothing or he releases more than we ask for, because we are only living for Him and for Him alone. Faith enables us to go places and do more for God.

Now look at when a plane is assembled correctly, all clean and shiny, but not moving anywhere because of the cost of fuel for the flights. God calls us to go into the world. We need to go and not stay in the same place all the time. But the plane remains at the airport all the time, never entering the sky and going to a new place. One is forever conscious of the cost of journeys and prefers not to go anywhere. Is this a blessing to God, when one is stationary all the time and never going anywhere? Or does God delight to see a church in action?

There was a time in my life when I had a picture. I saw many Christians standing on the beach with their fishing rods. They all went fishing and hoped to catch one or two fish that afternoon. There were two other Christians standing on the beach, next to a boat and a large fishing net. They were asking others to come and join them as they go deep into the water to catch a large number of fish. They received a lot of discouragement from others.

"It's safe here when we stand on the edge of the beach. If we go deep into the sea we can drown. I'm staying where I am."

"I have to submit to those in authority, and my minister has not told me to move, so I'm staying here."

"I'm used to catching fish this way and I know I will catch fish every week. I've never been in a boat and have no guarantee that I will catch any fish."

People continued to give one reason after another as to why they did not want to go deeper into the water.

The two Christians were reflecting on some scriptures, Mark 7v13, Numbers 13v33 and Hebrews 13v17 were just some of the verses they could see people clinging to, not able to let go of their fishing rods and get into the boat ready for a big catch. Tradition, feeling like grasshoppers and listening only to the one in authority (the minister) became reasons why people would not change their ways. Everyone wanted to keep hold of their own fishing rod.

Caution and protection may not allow people to go deeper with God and put chains around people's lives. Encouragement and faith equip people to read the Bible more, draw closer to God and realise what a mighty difference they can make for God and for others. People are searching for that encouragement to go deeper with God and get feel very discouraged when they hear the opposite in the church. "Others learn to be content with life. You need to learn to be content too!" they hear people say. It can seem like the whole church has lost its first love, and the Lord is telling the church to repent and the church is defending for its ways. "How frustrating when no one is listening", the person thinks.

When Apostles and Prophets are the foundation of every church, things will change in a very beautiful way for the church. Encouragement to go on with God will be the way in the church instead of caution and fear. Churches will remain committed to the vision instead of drifting and engaging in other things, and the Lord will build His church.

Chapter 15 – Pleasing God Above Man

We read this verse in the book of Galatians.

"Am I now trying to win the approval of human beings, or of God? Or am I trying to please people? If I were still trying to please people, I would not be a servant of Christ." Galatians 1v10 NIV

How do we know when to look to others and when to look to God alone? I thought about this very much, and God was showing me how relationships work in His kingdom. We are called to please God. We should never be pleasing man above God. What exactly does that mean?

I started to use my imagination. Could I say to my friend John that I will not give him a cup of coffee on Sunday? "I'll bless your wife and daughter but you can make one for yourself. I am not here to please you. I'm here to please God!" That is very unloving when I use the scriptures to ignore my brother John. So what does it mean to please God? Look at these scriptures:

"He who says he is in the light, and hates his brother, is in darkness until now." 1 John 2v9 NKJV

"Whoever hates his brother is a murderer, and you know that no murderer has eternal life abiding in him." 1 John 3v15 NKJV

"If someone says, "I love God," and hates his brother, he is a liar; for he who does not love his brother whom he has seen, how can he love God whom he has not seen?" 1 John 4v20 NKJV

We should love others. We should not hate anyone, as these scriptures tell us.

"Be devoted to one another in love. Honour one another above yourselves." Romans 12v10 NIV

"If it is possible, as far as it depends on you, live at peace with everyone." Romans 12v18 NIV

"By this everyone will know that you are my disciples, if you love one another." John 13v35 NIV

We are called to love one another, to be at peace with others, and to think of others above ourselves. How can we say to someone, 'I am not here to please you. I'm here to please God.' How can we say this? Surely when you please God then he longs for you to please one another. When you do something for someone else, you are doing it for God.

The King will reply, 'Truly I tell you, whatever you did for one of the least of these brothers and sisters of mine, you did for me.' Matthew 25v40

So should we always set out to please one another? Is that God's heart?

Look at these scriptures:

"If we are thrown into the blazing furnace, the God we serve is able to deliver us from it, and he will deliver us from Your Majesty's hand. But even if he does not, we want you to know, Your Majesty, that we will not serve your gods or worship the image of gold you have set up." Daniel 3v17-18 NIV

Then they said to the king, "Daniel, who is one of the exiles from Judah, pays no attention to you, Your Majesty, or to the decree you put in writing. He still prays three times a day." Daniel 6v13 NIV

But Peter and the *other* apostles answered and said: "We ought to obey God rather than men." Acts 5v29

Jesus turned and said to Peter, "Get behind me, Satan! You are a stumbling block to me; you do not have in mind the concerns of God, but merely human concerns." Matthew 16v23 NIV

Why did the three men refuse to obey the King? Why did Daniel not obey the law? Why did the Apostles continue to preach the gospel? Why did Jesus reject the words of Peter and say what he said? The people did not want to compromise with the things they were doing for God. They could not obey man when it would lead them to doing things that were outside God's will.

We need to realise that we too will not be able to please man when God is speaking in a different way.

When do we find ourselves in situations where we may please God in such a way that it does not please others? Here are four scriptures that show how someone always puts God above others in their lives.

1. We have faith to believe something will bless God and others do not have faith. Look at these verses.

Some of those present were saying indignantly to one another, "Why this waste of perfume? It could have been sold for more than a year's wages and the money given to the poor." And they rebuked her harshly. "Leave her alone," said Jesus. "Why are you bothering her? She has done a beautiful thing to me. Mark 14v4-6 NIV

The woman was showing her love to Jesus in a very beautiful way. Others were looking not at the woman but the jar of perfume and the material value of the jar.

2. We are ready to do something that others may not agree with.

When we heard this, we and the people there pleaded with Paul not to go up to Jerusalem. Then Paul answered, "Why are you weeping and breaking my heart? I am ready not only to be bound, but also to die in Jerusalem for the name of the Lord Jesus." Acts 21v12-13 NIV

Paul was ready to lay down his life for the work that God had put on his heart to do, even if it meant he would die. He loved God so much.

3. Our love for God and our heart for others is so deep that we will do things others may feel uneasy about.

"They all gave out of their wealth; but she, out of her poverty, put in everything—all she had to live on." Mark 12v44 NIV

People may think we will die because we have no money left to buy food, but there may come a time when one loves God so deeply that it is a delight to give everything to Him.

4. When we forgive someone and show love to them, and self-righteous people may feel this is unjust.

"The older brother became angry and refused to go in. So his father went out and pleaded with him." Luke 15v28 NIV

Some may say, "Reject that person. They squander whatever you give them. Don't let them waste your possessions." You may say, "I want to welcome them." Whom do you listen to, man or God?

There was a time when I thought about some personal experiences in my own life. I would choose to trust God and seek His face, and so I spent many hours alone in the presence of God reading the Bible and learning God's Word. But is this right? I thought about these scriptures a lot.

"Anyone who does not provide for their relatives, and especially for their own household, has denied the faith and is worse than an unbeliever." 1 Timothy 5v8 NIV

"For even when we were with you, we gave you this rule: "The one who is unwilling to work shall not eat." 2 Thessalonians 3v10 NIV

I chose to put God above even the one I love most of all on earth, my wife. I would spend long periods alone with God and not working to provide for my wife and children. But look at this verse.

"What I mean, brothers and sisters, is that the time is short. From now on those who have wives should live as if they do not." 1 Corinthians 7v29 NIV

Is this right? Surely our wife should be our greatest priority. The Bible gives a very clear instruction to every husband. "Husbands, love your wives, just as Christ loved the church and gave himself up for her." Ephesians 5v25 NIV

I had to be led by the Holy Spirit, and would choose to put God above even my own wife.

Many scriptures can be used to keep us within certain boundaries, but the truth is that God has much more for us. He wants to use us in new ways, in greater ways, so that we can reach more people with the good news. People may tell us to be wise, not foolish (Matthew 7v24-27), but God may tell us to be foolish (1 Corinthians 1v27), so that we trust Him in new ways.

The question is not 'what do we do' but 'why do we do it?' God looks at the motives of the heart – Proverbs 16v2. Are we doing something for the glory of God, serving out of a broken and contrite heart (Isaiah 57v15), or because we simply long for others to know Jesus, such that we love not our lives unto death (Revelation 12v11)? Are we ready to risk our lives for the sake of the gospel? Look at this verse in the book of Acts.

"Men who have risked their lives for the name of our Lord Jesus Christ." Acts 15v26 NKJV

So the question we have to ask ourselves is this. "How do we move from standing on the beach with our fishing rod to letting go, stepping into the boat, going deep into the sea and holding the net when it is thrown into the water?"

It begins in our heart. We have to be able to say that we are willing to change and that we want to go deeper with God. We have to be prepared for God to use us in a new way. Then we pray with a sincere heart and ask God to do something new in our lives. We tell God we want to draw closer to him, and God will start to work in our lives and lead us in a different way.

No longer do we look at things from the point of the law, but instead from a heart of love that is totally devoted to God. Love becomes the daily motive for every decision we make. We have only one reason to live every day and that is to serve God. "For me to live is Christ." We reach a point where that becomes our daily purpose for living. We live for Christ, and Christ alone. Why? Because of love.

Love is no longer something we learn about, but something we can personally testify to. We know God's love for us in such a deep and personal way that we just want to do all that we can to honour Him every single day. Pleasing God above man becomes a new way of living for us.

Chapter 16 – Loving Others

What about relationship with others? We are called to love one another as John 13v35 says. But what is our intention? What is our purpose in loving others?

Let's look at Jesus and Zacchaeus. Jesus loved Zacchaeus and said he was going to his house. Jesus entered the home of Zacchaeus. And Zacchaeus found salvation. Read these verses:

And Jesus said to him, "Today salvation has come to this house, because he also is a son of Abraham; for the Son of Man has come to seek and to save that which was lost." Luke 19v9-10

Jesus could have entered the home of Zacchaeus simply to talk about his past and his challenges he faced in his life. 'You know,

Zacchaeus, I am glad to be alive. I could have died when people tried to push me off a cliff (see Luke 4v29-30). But I'm glad to be alive. I really am.' But Jesus did not talk about his past. Instead he met with Zacchaeus who repented and found Salvation. Jesus was focussed on his purpose for meeting with Zacchaeus, the purpose of Salvation.

We can meet with others for a number of reasons.

1. To give them Salvation as Jesus did with Zacchaeus.
2. To bear their burdens as Galatians 6v2 says.
3. To build them up in the Word of God.
4. To receive from others so that we are personally built up.

Do we choose to meet simply to enjoy one another's company, or with a clear, specific goal that God has put on our hearts?

What is the eternal consequence of our choices? Shall we meet someone next week and just enjoy time with them? Or shall we meet with others to pray with them, like the people did in Acts 12v5, or to give them the gospel as Jesus did with Zacchaeus? What is our purpose in meeting, and what is the eternal consequence?

Naturally, God is always blessed when someone gives their life to Him. God desires that none should perish – 2 Peter 3v9. He does not want a single soul to perish. And when we give the gospel to someone, God is blessed. But God is also blessed when we build up others, and when we bear their burdens too.

Let's ask a couple of questions. If Salvation is the most important matter in our lives (following God and going to heaven instead of hell), then why is Jesus concerned about our earthly needs?

He answered and said to them, "He who has two tunics, let him give to him who has none; and he who has food, let him do likewise." Luke 3v11 NKJV

If Salvation is important, why does Jesus spend time speaking and listening to the people in the temple? Why didn't Jesus go into more homes like He did when he entered Zacchaeus' home?

"And it came to pass, that after three days they found him in the temple, sitting in the midst of the doctors, both hearing them, and asking them questions." Luke 2v46

Like Jesus, we can meet with people for different reasons. That is not a problem. But the question, which impacts our eternal life, is this. "What fruit do you intend to bear?" Look at this verse.

"Every branch in Me that does not bear fruit He takes away; and every *branch* that bears fruit He prunes, that it may bear more fruit." John 15v2 NKJV

Jesus wants us to bear more fruit in our lives. The question is, what is our aim, our purpose in our daily activities? Is it simply to relax and enjoy many blessings all the time for ourselves, or is it to see others come to Salvation? The more people we give the gospel to, the more we bless God. The more people we show love to (bearing their burdens), the more we bless God. The more we build up others, the more we bless God. But do we pray and go, with a clear intention, to do the work of God, or instead just meet simply because we like to be blessed in our lives? Is our focus on ourselves or on others?

When it is for others, God is blessed and will reward us for all eternity. When it is for ourselves, we live just like the unsaved do, trying to satisfy ourselves all the time. We may be good, but what are we actually seeking to do to please God? Or are we seeking just to please ourselves? Pleasing God is a blessing to Him and we will be increasing our eternal treasures. Pleasing ourselves makes us very much like the way non-Christians live and we may not have many eternal treasures. Choosing to bear fruit is such a blessing to God, but is that our purpose? Or do we just want to love others like the heathen do?

For if you love those who love you, what reward have you? Do not even the tax collectors do the same? And if you greet your brethren only what do you do more *than others?* Do not even the tax collectors do so? Matthew 5v46-47 NKJV.

"What reward will you have?" Jesus asks. Are we no different to the unsaved? Do we live our life with a clear objective, a clear purpose, or just go through life like the unsaved, but with the difference that we belong to a church? Is that really the only noticeable difference between a Christian and a non-Christian, that one attends church and the other does not?

A non-Christian may spend their spare time doing a lot of voluntary work. They get saved, give up their voluntary work and devote their spare time to the church instead. They have always had a pleasant character even before they were saved, so do they really need to read the Bible? At the end of the day, is there much difference between Christians and non-Christians apart from the fact that one group of people regularly attend church whilst the others do not?

Do we really want to enter heaven without any reward? The question Jesus asks is very important. 'What reward will you have?' He compares us to tax collections who also like to greet their friends. We, like tax collectors, are polite and greet others. Is there really anything that is different in us that should cause God to reward us? Or are we just drifting through life without any real purpose as a Christian?

With more and more revelations, I was realising there was so much God wanted to be taught. Jesus said to:

'Go therefore and make disciples of all the nations, baptizing them in the name of the Father and of the Son and of the Holy Spirit, *teaching them* to observe all things that I have commanded you. And lo, I am with you always, even to the end of the age." Matthew 28v18-20 NKJV

Do we realise how much there is to be taught? We are to teach *everything* the Bible commands us. In order to teach everything, we need to know everything.

Look at Acts 20v27:

"For I have not hesitated to proclaim to you the whole will of God." NIV

The Apostle Paul wanted to teach the *whole* of God's will and not just the majority of his ways. Remember, one sin, just one sin, can make us look as guilty as someone breaking the whole of God's laws says James.

God looks at everything in our hearts. He looks at our willingness to serve Him, our skills, talents and strengths and our weaknesses too. He looks at the sin inside us and refines us so that we are clean and beautiful in His eyes. Our motive (our reason for serving the Lord), is very important to God.

What is our motive for serving the Lord? What was my motive? Proverbs 16v2 tells us that God looks at the *motives* of our hearts. What is my motive for serving others?

Sometimes when I read a book a particular chapter, paragraph or sentence would really speak to me. I'd make a note of it so that I could refer to it next time I went away on mission. And I'd write down things for my own personal encouragement, so that I could be a blessing to God as I delight myself in Him (as Psalm 37v4 says). This is a note I once wrote from a book I read.

"If you want to walk on water you have to get out of the boat" by John Ortberg. Page 50 says, "What is my deepest dream?" It goes on to say, "If I had to name the one true thing that I believe I was set on this earth to do, what would it be?"

My reason for living is to bless God with my life and to please Him in every way. My deepest dream is to see people having a rich, eternal life in heaven. I do not want to see people suffering loss in heaven. I don't like poverty and do not want people to miss out on many eternal riches. I long to see everyone having an abundant life in heaven. I also know that God desires that none should perish, and I long to see people saved.

I cannot bear to see one child sleeping rough. I cannot bear to see one person injured after being knocked by a car and lying in the road. How much more can I not bear to see a person being thrown into the lake of fire. It's too unbearable. I must act now. That is why I have faith in God to believe He can enable me to reach the lost and that He *will* answer every single prayer. Because I believe, I will trust Him for much. I will not compare Him with anyone else (Isaiah 40v25). I know He can do more than I can ask or imagine, so I will pray and expect great things from God, so that others do not have to suffer in hell but can spend eternity in heaven, with many eternal riches.

This is what gives me both the motivation every day to read the Word of God and to share His Word with others. Some of the things I read like Matthew 7v13-14 I take very seriously, and long to see people not only on the road to heaven but also greatly rewarded in heaven. I would not want to see people suffering loss in heaven as 1 Corinthians 3v15 says when I believe everyone can have a wonderful, rich eternal life.

The devil wants us to decline to serve God so that souls do not hear the gospel and get saved. The devil will make us be glad just to enter heaven and escape hell. But God wants to reward us, and when we know how much God loves us and wants to give us for all eternity, may we become motivated to serve God all the time and see souls saved. We love others and want to see them not only saved but grow in their relationship with God, so that they too will be delighted to serve God all the time.

Chapter 17 – Conclusion

Different people can define being a Christian in a different way. Some say that to 'believe' in Jesus will get you into heaven. Others say that, when you show loyalty to a church, that is clear evidence that you are a Christian. The Bible tells us to love the Lord our God with all our heart, and I believe this is what God asks of us for all eternity. If we do not want to love Him with all our heart, will we enter heaven when we die? And as the first chapter shows, you cannot quantify love. There is no exact way to prove you are completely devoted to God.

You, and only you, can decide how you want to love God. You can measure your love for God in many different ways. But the question, at the end of the day, is how do you interpret the scriptures? How do you understand the word 'love'? The greatest commandment is to love the Lord your God with all your heart – Mark 12v30. You alone know your heart and whether you really want to follow God and serve Him every moment of your life.

How do you define love? How do you quantify love? How do you define when a cup of coffee is now cold? After 11 minutes? After 12 minutes and 20 seconds? How do you measure something?

The devil can make us all look at others around us and think that we are OK. If we see 99 cups of cold coffee in the room and we offer someone a cup of cold coffee, do we feel bad? Well, all the other cups of coffee are cold, so I don't see what the problem is with my contribution. But only by reading the Bible and really taking note of what Jesus asks of us can we get to know if we are honouring God in every way in our life.

You have to look at yourself and ask many questions. Do I really want to love God with all my heart, or am I reluctant and hesitant to love Him completely? Do I prefer to be partially committed to God? Do I just want to give to God the very minimum in order to ensure I avoid hell and enter heaven?

Do I really want to bless God all the time so that nothing is burnt up on judgment day? Do I really want to have many treasures in heaven for all eternity? Only you can make the decision. How much do you want to enjoy serving God? How much do you want to enjoy a wonderful relationship with Him? How much do you want to know the Word of God so that the scriptures become a wonderful testimony in your life, and you can tell yourself, with absolute confidence, that you know God, because your relationship is so strong? You once believed the promises of God, but now you know them and can testify to them in your own life. You really know that God will always provide, even when it looks as though the provisions are about to end

– see 1 Kings 17v12. You know the power of God. Matthew 22v29 was once a verse you believed but now you know it is true because you personally know the power of God.

"Jesus answered and said to them, "You are mistaken, not knowing the Scriptures nor the power of God." Matthew 22v29 NKJV

You have to choose. How much do you want to love God? How much do you want to know God? Do you want to take a chance and hope that you know God and totally love Him, or would you like to be sure? You can go to church and serve, and quite honestly, you can live very much like a non-Christian. You convince yourself that you are going to heaven because you go to church. But, are you willing to seek the Lord and read the Bible and really know the truth for yourself so that you can be absolutely confident you love God with all your heart and know Him?

There is a song we sing called "How deep the Fathers love for us." It is based on 1 John 3v1. Could we sing a new song – 'How deep is my love for my Father. It's vast, beyond all measure." Could we sing that from the bottom of our heart? The deeper the love, the greater the sacrificial love we have for God every day, the richer will our eternal life be in heaven. No longer will things become an effort to do but a delight, knowing just how much our life is a mighty blessing to God and will one day be richly rewarded.

Love should be the motive in absolutely everything we do. We can do so much for God and have a very blessed eternal life. A very blessed life. Or we can enter heaven with no rewards and suffer loss, or we can even enter hell if we do not obey God and refuse to repent.

Think about some of the ways you can bless God. Imagine, on a Sunday morning, inviting others to come and join you from 6am to 8am just to memorise the Bible. Each Sunday you read the same scriptures over and over again until you know them and do not even need to open the Bible. You read Psalm 117 again and again until you know the Psalm completely. Another Sunday you read Psalm 15 verses 1-3 over and over again until you know the verses. You say one verse without looking at the Bible, then read the other two verses. You then see if you can say two verses without looking at the Bible, and eventually all three verses. You can now quote Psalm 15v1-3 without opening the Bible. Well done. How much would this bless God for all eternity?

Could you see God welcoming people into heaven, then suddenly looking at you and being still? He hugs you for 15 minutes and says, "You blessed me so much, encouraging many people to memorize the Word of God. You blessed me in a very wonderful way." How do you feel for God to choose you out of a number of people and give you a hug for 15 minutes? Not a hug for one minute or two, but for fifteen minutes. Would you really love to be esteemed by God on judgment day and blessed for all eternity?

I look back to 2017. The UK had decided to leave the EU (European Union) and now had to agree the way to depart from the EU. Imagine if a church had said, "This is such an important time for the UK that for the next 21 days we shall open the church for prayer from 5am to 8am every day. We shall pray and fast for 21 days. Please join us at every opportunity to pray for the UK government at this time." How blessed God would be to see the church praying for the government. What could his reaction be on judgment day? A fifteen minute hug for you personally for praying during the 21 days? What a blessing. God is blessed when we lay down our lives and He simply cannot fail to notice our hearts and one day give us a reward.

An intellectual Christian can say that fasting is not essential to get into heaven, nor is an early morning prayer meeting. However, a

Christian who delights in honouring God may be very pleased to organise such a meeting when a nation such as the UK is going through very big changes such as leaving the EU.

Do we look at God, or money? Someone who looks at God may be glad to organise a meeting simply because He wants God's ways for the nation. Someone who looks at money will look at the cost of organising the 21 day event and wonder if the church can cover the cost for the extra electricity being used? Where is our focus? On God's heart and his promises such as Luke 6v38, or on the bank account and the amount of funds required to put on such meetings in the church? Let love be the motive, and always stand on God's promises. Take every opportunity to bless God and be a living sacrifice for Him as Romans 12v1 says. (NIV). Do everything out of a heart of love for God. Always put God first. Always.

The devil is very subtle and clever. He can make us think that as long as we are in unity with others, we have to be doing the right thing so it's OK. But is that always the case? Or as long as we 'obey our church leader' then obviously we are being a good Christian. But will we enter heaven when we die if we base our thoughts on just a few facts? Or is there more that God is looking for?

Just what do we have to do to enter heaven? And is heaven really the same for everybody? Or could God have such an abundance of eternal treasures that He would love to give us on judgement day for all eternity? Does a church service have to be mundane and boring, or can it be led out of a heart of joy and delight all the time as we get such joy from doing things for Jesus? What exactly is our first love?

Why did Jesus tell us to store up treasures in heaven? See Matthew 6v20. Surely getting to heaven and escaping hell is what matters most of all, so what's the relevance of eternal treasures?

It's very easy to say that we would rather be poor in heaven than enter hell, but no one would want to suffer loss in heaven. We all enjoy blessings. Can you imagine drinking water every day in heaven for all eternity whilst others enjoy apple juice, mango juice, passion fruit and many other beautiful drinks? Have you ever given thought to what it could mean to suffer loss?

Can you imagine being told by Jesus to depart because he never knew you? You were loyal to the church but never had an intimate relationship with God?

May you come to have a deep, rich, intimate relationship with God. May you love Jesus more than any other, so much more than anything.

Let's end by looking at these two songs:

As the deer pants for the water
So my soul longs after You
You alone are my heart desire
And I long to worship You

You're my friend
And You are my brother
Even though you are the King
I love you more than any other
So much more than anything

Think about these words, especially the words in italics. Let us love God more than any other; so much more than anything.

When I survey the wondrous cross
On which the Prince of glory died

My richest gain I count but loss
And pour contempt on all my pride

Where every realm of nature mine
My gift was still be far too small
Love so amazing, so divine
Demands my soul, my life, my all

Let us give ourselves all to Jesus. Let us build a very rich relationship with God. Devote yourself to God all the time. Get to know Him more and more. Delight in serving Him. Choose to love God more than any other, so much more than anything. Decide that the love of God is so amazing, so divine that I, in return, simply want to give him my soul, my life, my all.

Remember, there are two places everyone can go to when they die, heaven or hell. I pray that the second of these two verses be our testimony:

And then I will declare to them, 'I never knew you; depart from Me, you who practice lawlessness!' Matthew 7v23 NKJV

For our citizenship is in heaven, from which we also eagerly wait for the Saviour, the Lord Jesus Christ. Philippians 3v20 NKJV

And may we not only enter heaven, but also receive an abundance of eternal riches, which are ours to keep forever and ever. May the Lord reward us so greatly on judgment day.

About the Author

Richard Smart had attended church all his life and became a Christian at the age of 11. However, since his marriage to Corrol he has desired to learn more and more about God and has spent a lot of hours reading the Bible to know the Lord more, as well as reading a lot of Christian materials. Richard has a deep desire to see others know God in a very beautiful relationship and for the last twenty years he's made regular mission trips to East Africa to teach the Word of God. Richard and his wife have two children.

Email: richcorrol@gmail.com

Richard Smart

Thank you for reading my book!

I appreciate and welcome your constructive feedback.

Please would you leave a positive review on the platform where you bought it, to let me know what you thought and found useful.

Thank you, God bless you,

– Richard Smart